THE POLITICS OF
IMMIGRATION AND RA

THE POLITICS OF
IMMIGRATION AND RACE

ANDREW GEDDES

baseline
BOOKS

First published 1996 by
Baseline Book Company
PO Box 34
Chorlton
Manchester M21 9LL

British Library Cataloguing in Publication Data

ISBN 1 897626 09 6

Cover design   Ian Price
Cover illustration   Min Cooper
Typesetting   Kathryn Holliday
Printed and bound by Nuffield Press, Abingdon

ACKNOWLEDGEMENTS

I would like to thank Bob Carter, Jo-Ann Cundill and Steven Fielding for comments. Any remaining errors of fact or interpretation are mine. **AG**

CONTENTS

TABLES & FIGURES

ABBREVIATIONS

BfV	Bundesamt für Verfassungschutz
BUF	British Union of Fascists
CARD	Campaign Against Racial Discrimination
CLPD	Campaign for Labour Party Democracy
CRC	Community Relations Commission
CRE	Commission for Racial Equality
DVU	Deutsche Volksunion
EU	European Union
EVW	European Volunteer Workers
FN	Front National
GLC	Greater London Council
JCAR	Joint Campaign Against Racialism
LFS	Labour Force Survey
LPRAG	Labour Party Race Action Group
NCCI	National Committee for Commonwealth Immigrants
NEC	National Executive Committee
NF	National Front
NPD	Nationaldemokratische Partei Deutschlands
PR	proportional representation
RRB	Race Relations Board
SEA	Single European Act
TEU	Treaty on European Union

INTRODUCTION

Immigration, ideas of 'race' and supposed 'racial' differences are at the very heart of contemporary British politics. In order to analyse their significance at the end of the 1990s, this book investigates four key issues. The first is why questions of immigration, race and racism have become such important aspects of social and political debate in Britain. The second is factors which have underpinned the development of policy responses to 'problems' of racism and immigration in the post-war period. The third is the effects these policy responses have had on 'ethnic minority' political participation in Britain. The fourth is the effects of immigration and racism on political systems in other European countries, and indeed on the European Union (EU) as a whole.

'PROBLEMS' OF IMMIGRATION AND RACE

In investigating these inter-related themes, this book pays a good deal of attention to the 'problems' raised by immigration and the politics of race and racism in post-war Britain. However, rather than accept the policy framework as given, it attempts to explore the assumptions which have underpinned policy development under both Conservative and Labour governments. This means that the book pays particular attention to the problematisation of immigration issues. The way in which social and political issues are defined as problems affects attempts to solve them.

Perceptions of immigration have played an important part in the process of issue problematisation. Even though immigrants have made an important contribution to economic prosperity in Britain and other west European countries since the end of the second world war, a 'negative ideology' of immigration undermines attempts to construct a policy framework whereby immigrants and their descendants may be effectively incorporated into west European societies.[1]

In fact, the very term 'immigrant' could be held to be misleading in a British context. Many people who came to live in Britain moved from former colonies and came as *citizens*. This meant that they had the same formal rights and duties as all other British citizens, even though they may not have been able properly to exercise those rights. The children of immigrants (and their children) were actually born and raised in Britain and are in no sense immigrants. That is why this book pays particular attention to issues of citizenship and explores these issues in a European context.

Issues associated with immigration and, more recently, asylum, were salient features of British and European political debates during 1995. In Britain, the Conservative government introduced proposals for further tightening of the already restrictive procedures for asylum-seekers. It was also noted, by a former director of the Conservatives' research department, that immigration issues 'played well on the doorsteps' during the 1994 European elections campaign. In addition, at the December 1995 Madrid meeting of EU heads of government, the British blocked a proposal from the European Commission which sought to tighten EU anti-racism laws. Instead, a less ambitious declaration was agreed. In taking these, and other steps, the Conservative government contends that it is seeking to improve 'race relations'. Whether or not this is the case, and there are reasons for supposing it to be unlikely, it is very important that the assumptions underpinning race relations policy are explored. It is also necessary to assess the effects of policy on the operation of the political process.

THE ARGUMENT OF THIS BOOK

The central argument advanced in this book is that the nature of party debates on immigration-related issues in the 1960s has had adverse effects on ethnic minority political participation in the 1980s and 1990s. Recent increases in ethnic minority representation in political institutions such as local councils and the House of Commons should not disguise the marked under-representation that exists. Political scientists often focus on the question 'who gets what, when and how?' as a way of understanding the decision-making process. This book demonstrates that a necessary prior question is 'who participates?'. If ethnic minorities are excluded from the decision-making process, then under-representation is likely to engender continued marginalisation.

However, before considering the formulation of what is known as race relations policy in the 1960s, and assessing its participatory effects, it is important to provide some conceptual and historical contextualisation.

In Chapter 1 key terms such as 'race', 'ethnicity' and 'citizenship' are introduced. Particular attention is paid to ideas of citizenship, as well as to the important distinction between *access to* and *utilisation of* citizenship rights.

Chapter 2 illustrates Britain's long historical experience of immigration, and shows that we can draw parallels between treatment of Irish and Jewish people in the late nineteenth century and treatment of immigrants from Asia, Africa and the Caribbean after the second world war. In the two cases there are elements of commonality in perception of the immigration 'problem'. In Victorian times, as today, immigrants were often seen as the cause of social problems and served as convenient scapegoats for what were in reality more complex issues.

The social demographic status of Britain's ethnic minorities is outlined in Chapter 3. By analysing patterns of settlement, employment, socioeconomic status, education and housing, important aspects of social inequality in Britain may be set in their proper context. The chapter also demonstrates the need to refine terms such as 'black' and 'ethnic minority' to take account of differential performance in certain sectors by some ethnic minority groups.

In Chapter 4 factors underpinning development of British race relations policy are assessed. The chapter looks in particular at the motives of the dominant Conservative and Labour parties in supporting a policy framework which sought to restrict numbers of immigrants whilst, at the same time, introducing measures designed to combat aspects of racism. It reveals that Labour had most to lose from politicisation of immigration-related issues, being fearful that if it was seen as being 'soft' on immigration it would lose votes to the Conservatives.

Following this, Chapters 5 and 6 explore debates within the two main political parties more fully. They analyse the repoliticisation of immigration and race relations by Margaret Thatcher after her election as Conservative party leader in 1975, and consider whether playing the 'race card' helped the Conservatives to win the 1979 general election. They also investigate criticism in the 1970s of the Labour leadership's support for race relations policy by increasingly radicalised party members who were disillusioned by what they saw as concessions to racism. An important aspect of this critique was the controversial debate about black sections.

Having looked at the formation of policy, as well as at inter- and intra-party debates, the book turn its attention to ethnic minority political participation. Chapter 7 explores factors explaining increased representation, as well as reasons for continued under-representation. It also pays some attention to informal political participation which, some would suggest, is becoming increasingly important.

Finally, in Chapter 8, developments in Britain are placed in a European context. In particular, the politics of immigration in France and Germany are analysed. The chapter reveals that there are major differences in policy responses to 'problems' of immigration in all three countries. It argues that differing traditions of citizenship and nationhood, as well as other aspects of historical particularity, help to explain these differences. The chapter also looks at the development of EU immigration policy to determine how common responses to issues of immigration are being formulated at supranational level. The argument that a 'fortress Europe' is being created, within which national policy emphases on tight immigration control are writ large at European level, is assessed.

NOTE

1 M Livi-Bacci, 'South-North Migration: A Comparative Approach to North American and European Experiences', *The Changing Course of International Migration* (OECD, Paris, 1993).

1 IDEAS OF RACE AND BELONGING

Four terms are central to this book and are explored in this chapter. It assesses first what meaning, if any, can be attached to the linked ideas of *race* and *racism*, and examines how bogus notions of racial superiority and inferiority can fuel racist political ideologies. Secondly it considers *ethnicity* and analyses factors which condition the relationship between ethnic minorities and majorities and lead majority ethnic groups, on occasion, to establish social, political and economic boundaries which exclude minorities. Ethnic origin can serve as the basis for social exclusion, but it is the status attached to *citizenship* which in a formal and legal sense tells us who is or is not a member of a particular society. The concept of citizenship has particular relevance to the issues of political participation which are examined later in this book. This chapter therefore asks what it is to be a citizen and what citizenship entails. Finally the chapter considers whether, as some claim, anti-racism and struggles for equality can be described as 'politically correct'.

RACE AND RACISM

It might seem strange to begin a book by stating what it is not about, but in the context of the following chapters it is important to do just this. This book is not about race in any scientific or biological sense, because there is no evidence to suggest that human beings can be categorised according to racial origin. There is only one race that matters, and that is the human race. Ideologies that claim otherwise are flawed and can, as lessons from recent history (such as the second world war) show, lead to extremes of oppression, misery, murder and, at their worst, genocide.

However, if the concept of race can make no scientific contribution to explaining human behaviour, why have appeals to supposed racial origin been powerful mobilising forces in contemporary politics? Why do some people act as though notions of racial difference actually have a substantive basis? In fact, these questions go to the heart of sociological analyses of race and racism. In this context it is helpful to consider a scientist's frustration about spurious use of racial categories:

In fact, as a geneticist, I believed that, thanks to biology, I could help people see things more clearly by saying, 'You talk about race, but what does the word mean?' And I showed them it couldn't be defined without arbitrariness or ambiguity... In other words, there is no scientific basis for the concept of race and, as a result, racism must disappear. A few years ago, I would have argued that in making that statement I had properly discharged my role as a scientist and a citizen. And yet, though there are no *races*, racism certainly exists![1]

This quotation illustrates two important points. First, it demonstrates that even though there is no credible scientific evidence to support the view that human beings can be grouped according to race, some people continue to act as if this is possible. As a result, social and biological issues become conflated and the former are linked to misconceived notions of the latter. As Guillaumin puts it, 'Imaginary and real races play the same role in the social process and are therefore identical as regards their social function: this is precisely the sociological problem.'[2] Second, it makes abundantly clear the need in addressing sociological problems of race and racism to examine how supposed racial differences are given social and political meaning. That is, it focuses debate on ways in which ideas of racial 'otherness' and 'difference' are constructed.

Analysis of alleged racial differences increased during the nineteenth century as matters such as skin pigmentation, eye and hair colour, and skull size were measured by eugenicists attempting to construct racial hierarchies. Analysis of racism is a more recent phenomenon. It developed in the period between the first and second world wars, and was given particular momentum by the genocidal actions of the Nazis who used false notions of racial difference to murder millions of people they considered to be inferior.

There is clearly an important link between race and racism because 'without racism physical characteristics are devoid of social significance'.[3] However, it is quite difficult to provide a definition of racism because sociologists dispute the various meanings that can be attached to the term. Generally, racism is held to comprise utilisation of biological, genetic or phenotypical differences, such as skin colour, to discriminate between people. These differences are often the basis on which claims about the behaviour of racially-defined groups and stereotypes are constructed. This definition incorporates both the anti-black racism we see in Britain and other European countries, and anti-Semitism.

However, although the main focus of this book's analysis is Britain, we should note that the terms we employ to analyse issues of race and racism in Britain would not necessarily be used in other European countries. In Britain, analysis focuses on what is called race relations policy and on the social position of ethnic minorities. In France and Germany, by contrast, such terms are not employed when analysing the effects of immigration. The French believe British race relations policy potentially to constitute a form of apartheid because of the emphasis it places on alleged racial differences. Germans do not even officially recognise that theirs is a country of immigration, while the legacy of their Nazi past makes analysis of race very sensitive. These differences are explored more fully in Chapter 8.

In Britain, racism is often analysed as an anti-black phenomenon targeted on post-war immigrants from South Asia, Africa and the Caribbean. Anti-black racism often centres on skin colour as a marker for bogus notions of superiority and inferiority. However, Chapter 2 will show that parallels can be drawn between hostility towards Irish and Jewish settlers at the turn of the twentieth century and hostility towards black immigrants after the second world war.

In addition to physical distinctions which serve as the basis of racism, it has also been argued that cultural differences are important. Social groups with their distinct cultural backgrounds, which they seek to maintain, may be viewed as a threat to social cohesion by the majority population. Minority cultures, and by clear implication those who espouse them, may also be viewed as inferior. The reaction to publication of Salman Rushdie's *The Satanic Verses*, the Gulf War and the rise of Islamic fundamentalism, has led to an increased awareness of British Muslims who, as a consequence of their cultural distinctness, have been perceived in some quarters as a 'threat' to British society. During the Gulf War the editor of the right-wing *Daily Star* in a particularly virulent outburst called for Muslims opposed to war in the Gulf to be 'kicked out' of Britain because they were 'a poisonous bunch of minority malcontents'.[4]

In broad terms it is possible to distinguish two main ways in which racism is propagated: informal or individual, and structural or institutional means. These two broadly distinguished forms of racism are, of course, interlinked and it is difficult effectively to oppose one without also confronting the other. On the individual level, racism is sometimes held to be 'unconscious' and deriving from 'common sense' assumptions about people based upon false racial differences. It is also often motivated by fear which can then fuel hatred. Some poor white people feel that they have most to lose to immigrants because of their own precarious social position. To them immigrants pose a threat to their employment and housing prospects. On the basis of this fear, racial hatred could develop. It is often held that individualised racism can be tackled by laws that prohibit racist activities and by education policies that emphasise toleration of difference. Institutional racism is held to be rooted in economic, political and social structures, and is not 'unconscious'. Instead, it can be knowingly exploited by power-holders in society to justify their positions and preserve their dominance. Radical writers have argued that racist ideologies can serve as the basis for state action.[5] Immigration controls introduced in the 1960s and 1970s have been seen as taking discrimination 'out of the market place' and giving it 'the sanction of the state' through legislation which made racism 'respectable and clinical' by institutionalising it.[6]

Perceptions of racism have an effect on policy. British anti-racism policy is largely informed by liberal ideas which focus on law and education as means of countering racist attitudes held to be largely individualised. Radicals argue that anti-racism needs to pay much closer attention to structural forms of racism and ways in which social institutions can themselves be racist.

It is thus evident that alleged racial differences are given meaning in particular social and political contexts – as constructs – and that in a biological or scientific sense notions of race have no explanatory value. This means that the use of racial categories to explain social and political behaviour needs to be rejected. Instead, analysis must focus on ways in which social and political circumstances give meaning to ideas of racial difference and racism.

The idea of race is clearly extremely problematic. Some argue that analysts who refer to racial differences risk legitimising an analytically empty notion. This has led some social scientists to problematise the term 'race' by placing it in inverted commas.

ETHNICITY AND ETHNIC MINORITIES

Like ideas of racial difference, those of ethnic belonging have been powerful influences on contemporary politics. Across central and eastern Europe following the end of the cold war, long submerged ethnic divisions have re-emerged. In Britain, policy makers formulate policy responses to issues raised by ethnic minorities. Similarly, ethnic minority political participation is a topic that has excited the interest of political scientists and is an issue addressed by this book.

In Britain ethnic minorities are typically held to be people of immigrant origin from, in particular, South Asia, Africa and the Caribbean. For the first time, the 1991 Census asked a question about ethnic origin (see Chapter 3). It categorised about 5.5 per cent of the British population as members of a minority ethnic group.

Ethnicity is often seen as a sense of group belonging based on shared interpretations of history, culture, traditions and experience. Ethnic identities can serve as the basis of both inclusion and exclusion by defining who can be a group member and who cannot. Phenotypical differences of skin colour may also be used to signify ethnic belonging, leading to supposed racial differences. Ethnicity can be expressed through protection and promotion of ethnic cultures as a way of celebrating the durable phenomenon of ethnic belonging. It can also be a way for ethnic minority groups to preserve a measure of autonomy and prevent incorporation into the norms of the majority culture.

However, ethnicity is not something that only minority groups have. Everybody has ethnicity. People talk of ethnic restaurants or ethnic shops to distinguish an Indian restaurant and a Latin American craft shop from a fish and chip shop and Marks & Spencer. Yet all four are expressive of ethnic identities. The point is that people tend to attribute ethnicity to minorities without noting that other organisations and institutions can be equally expressive of the ethnic identity of a majority group.

Ethnic identity can be a powerful political force, both positively and negatively. Positively, a shared ethnic origin can serve as a vehicle for expression of political rights, such as freedom of expression and self-determination. Negatively, ethnic difference can be used as the basis for oppression of one group by another. It plays an important part in generating notions of belonging, and can serve as the basis for inclusion and exclusion when ethnic origin – in particular minority and majority status – plays a part in the allocation of power. This allocation can have the effect of enforcing the dominance of one group over others.

In Britain the term 'black' is often used to distinguish ethnic minorities from the majority 'white' population. The term unites diverse ethnic communities in the face of common experiences of discrimination and oppression and is thus seen by some as a political colour signifying resistance to racism. In the Labour Party in the 1980s there was much debate about whether black people – meaning people of Asian or Afro-Caribbean origin – should be allowed to organise their own separate section within the party. Ultimately permission was refused.

In some senses it seems meaningful to distinguish the black population from the white population when account is taken of evidence of discrimination in many areas of society, such as immigration law, (un)employment, housing, the judicial process, education and the political system. The notion of 'black' is based on a politics of anti-racism as a way of generating a sense of common interest and solidarity and of developing communities of resistance to white racism.

In other ways it seems more difficult to use the term. Some argue that there are no common or shared interests that can form the basis for effective mobilisation of black people. There are divisions between people of Asian, African and Caribbean origin as well as within these very broadly defined groups. Indeed, many people of Asian origin do not recognise themselves as black and consider that black identities are more reflective of people of African and Caribbean origin. On this basis, some writers have recently paid increased attention to the experience of British Asians, particularly Muslims, since the controversy over Salman Rushdie's *The Satanic Verses*.[7]

Another important issue is whether black identities can serve as the basis for formal political mobilisation within the institutional and party structures of the political system at local and national level (as opposed to within more informal, perhaps community-based, organisations). The evidence tends to suggest that this is unlikely for three main reasons.

First, the formal political process seems to be unresponsive to black people. The number of black MPs in the House of Commons – six (out of 651) – is clear evidence of exclusion. If there is discrimination in the formal political process then the chances of successful political mobilisation are reduced. Liberals argue that it is only through participation within the existing institutions of the formal political process that exclusion can be combated and overcome. Radicals contend that far more fundamental change is needed in society if institutional racism is to be ended.

Second, many problems are not related to ethnicity or race but to socio-economic status. This does not mean that ethnic groups can be neatly merged into a class-based analysis of society and social inequality, because experience of racism distinguishes the experience of ethnic minorities. What it does mean is that existing political organisations that address socio-economic inequalities can serve, to some extent, as vehicles for political mobilisation. Voters of Asian or Afro-Caribbean origin are very strongly aligned with the Labour Party. This has as much to do with socio-economic status as with ethnicity.

Finally, the British political system is not responsive to ethnic-based political organisations. In Britain, third parties have always had problems establishing themselves because of the way in which the first-past-the-post electoral system discriminates against smaller parties. There have been no successful ethnic minority political parties in Britain. At the 1992 general election, for example, the Islamic Party made almost no impression in the constituencies it contested.

CITIZENSHIP

Notions of ethnic and racial difference can serve as the basis for social inclusion and exclusion. In formal legal terms, the clearest way of determining who does and who does not belong is through citizenship and nationality laws. Citizenship can be seen as meaning membership of a community. This communitarian perspective emphasises ways in which citizens are given rights which allow them to participate in key areas of social life, such as the political process.

Citizenship is usually linked closely to nation states, although the supranational EU now has (limited) provisions for citizenship rights for nationals of member states. Almost every person in the world is a citizen of one state or another. To be stateless is likely to be a serious predicament.

For many years, Britain had an 'imperial' notion of citizenship, even though, British people are, in fact, *subjects* of the Crown. The British Nationality Act 1948 reaffirmed the right of citizens of Britain's colonies and the newly-emerging Commonwealth to settle in Britain. British citizenship was based on imperial connections and ties to the 'mother' country. A feature of post-war British immigration is that many of those who came did so as citizens with associated rights and duties.

Over time, successive British governments have watered down, and finally abandoned, this imperial form of citizenship. From 1962 onwards a series of laws reduced the numbers of immigrants from the 'New Commonwealth' – countries such as India and African former colonies – and Pakistan, but did not restrict the entry rights of immigrants from the 'Old Commonwealth' – Canada, Australia and New Zealand – where most people were white. The British Nationality Act 1981 made close ties to Britain the qualification for citizenship and finally closed the door to immigrants from many former colonies who were no longer entitled to move to Britain.

There is, though, more to citizenship than formal ascription of membership through nationality laws. Attached to citizenship are rights and duties, such as the rights to vote and to receive social benefits and the duties to obey the law and, in some countries, do national service. In the early 1950s TH Marshall wrote what is often seen as the classic text on modern forms of citizenship. He focused particularly on Britain, though his analysis does have relevance for other economically developed liberal democracies. For him, citizenship is composed of three forms of rights:

- **legal** equal status before the law
- **political** equal access to political rights, such as voting
- **social** equal access to the services offered by the welfare state, such as social security, education and housing.

Marshall noted a progressive extension of these rights. The granting of legal rights in the eighteenth and nineteenth centuries created pressure for political rights which led, in the late nineteenth century, to enfranchisement of the male working class and, in the twentieth century, to votes for women. The development of political rights in turn increased demands for social rights because the working classes supported and participated in political organisations, such as the Labour Party and trade unions, which sought a more equitable distribution of economic resources and saw creation of a welfare state as one way to secure this.

Marshall held the extension of citizenship to the working classes to be a way of securing cultural integration which would foster a 'direct sense of community membership based on loyalty to a civilisation which is a common possession'.[8] However, this method of integration may not be particularly satisfactory for the working classes, who may wish to preserve aspects of their distinct cultural forms of belonging. It is even more problematic for members of minority ethnic communities who wish to maintain distinct cultural identities. It has been argued that group-differentiated rights are needed if a fully integrative form of citizenship is to be developed which reflects multi-ethnicity, promotes acceptance of minorities and encourages social and political inclusion of minority groups.[9]

There is also an important difference between *extension* and *utilisation* of rights. In a strict legal sense all individuals have equal rights and institutions exist to protect these rights. However, the possession of rights does not necessarily mean that they can be properly used. Racial discrimination means that black people may not receive equal treatment from the legal system, may face exclusion from the political process and may not be able effectively to utilise their social rights.

Building a genuine notion of community, and effective citizenship within it, seems to be dependent on all individuals being equally able to exercise their rights. Issues of citizenship are central to analyses of the politics of immigration, race and ethnicity and thus to generation of notions of belonging and non-belonging.

POLITICAL CORRECTNESS AND ANTI-ANTI-RACISM

The basic principles of liberal democracy imply equal rights for all citizens irrespective of such things as social class, gender, religion and ethnic origin. Access to citizenship is thus important, as are equal rights for citizens. Yet sometimes those who advocate equal rights are rather disparagingly labelled as 'politically correct', as though in some bizarre way the idea that all citizens should have equal rights is a passing fad. It is in fact a central tenet of a liberal democratic political system, such as the British, and is thus 'correct' in a very profound sense.

In Britain, policy has historically sought to secure equality of opportunity and thereby to create what has been called a 'level playing field' for all, regardless of ethnic origin. This response is firmly couched within the liberal tradition with its emphasis on the individual and faith in the responsiveness of the political system. Since the 1960s there has been an increase in organisations and pressure groups seeking racial equality. The Race Relations Act 1965 created the Race Relations Board. In 1968 the Community Relations Commission (CRC) was established. In 1976 the Commission for Racial Equality (CRE) was given powers to investigate alleged incidences of racism. Many local authorities, most famously the Greater London Council (GLC) in the early 1980s, have taken steps to tackle racism.

Advocates of equality have, however, come under attack. In recent years there has been a backlash against what has been called the race relations 'industry'. Some argue that Britain is a tolerant country and that advocates of racial equality are actually seeking to promote ideas that would have as their consequence an undesirable and radical transformation of British society. Anti-anti-racists, therefore, propagate a 'conservative' critique of race relations and seek to maintain what they perceive to be British traditions.

Individuals of this persuasion have in fact found it hard to reconcile themselves to the effects of immigration since the second world war, and would prefer that black British citizens, particularly those who are culturally distinct, adopt their own conservative interpretation of the cultural norms of the host population rather than seek to maintain their cultures. In their view this form of assimilation is most likely to lead to the kind of social cohesion they desire. Former cabinet minister Norman Tebbit postulated the so-called 'cricket test' when he asked: 'What side do they cheer for? Are you still harking back to where you came from or where you are?' Aside from the facile 'my country, right or wrong' aspect of these comments, they also draw attention to the essential 'Englishness' of many conservative notions of national identity. Scots, for example, are British, but they may not want to cheer for the English cricket team. In fact they may revel in its defeats.

The multi-ethnicity of British society is clearly evident and has been so for much longer than the post-war period which is the main focus of this book. Substantial numbers of British citizens who belong to minority ethnic groups have full formal rights. There is a powerful argument that the protection of the rights of ethnic minorities is an important, though neglected, part of liberal political theory and should be translated into practice by liberal democracies.

This implies that ethnic minorities are fully entitled to express cultural distinctness if they so choose, provided that they remain within the law, as well as to have equal access to political and social rights. Indeed, this principle was implicit in the creation of what is known in Britain as race relations policy. In 1966 home secretary Roy Jenkins described the goal of policy thus: 'Not a flattening process of assimilation but as equal opportunity accompanied by cultural diversity in an atmosphere of mutual tolerance.' Yet despite these seeming good intentions there is still evidence of racism in contemporary Britain which means that even though legal, political and social rights are formally extended they may not be effectively utilised.

Unequal citizenship poses a major challenge to the effectiveness of liberal democracy. One key aspect of this challenge is the responsiveness of the British political system to excluded groups, such as ethnic minorities. In later chapters the distinction between extension and utilisation of citizenship rights is developed more fully in an analysis of the participatory effects of British race relations policy and the extent of ethnic minority political participation.

KEY TERMS AND CONCEPTS

A discussion of key terms and concepts serves an important purpose in exploding the notion that biological or scientific explanations can make any contribution to analysis of the politics of immigration and race. Rather, what we need to investigate are ways in which notions of racial difference are given social and political meaning and then used to include certain groups and exclude others on the basis of supposed racial characteristics.

It is also important to bear in mind the fact that forms of racial and ethnic exclusion are inextricably linked to other forms of social inequality. In particular, class and gender inequalities play important parts in generating social differences. A thorough analysis of alleged racial differences must consider differences of social class and gender, among others.

This book pays particular attention to key issues associated with citizenship. It looks, for example, at the extension and utilisation of political rights. This entails analysis of the response of the British political system to immigration as well as of the attitudes of political parties. It is, however, important to provide analysis with an historical context. The next chapter assesses the extent to which responses to post-war immigration have been shaped by British experiences of earlier patterns of immigration and the legacy of Empire.

NOTES

1. A Jacquard, quoted in M Wieviorka, *The Arena of Racism* (Sage, London, 1995), p1.

2. C Guillaumin, quoted in ibid.

3. P van den Berghe, *Race and Racism* (John Wiley, New York, 1978), p11.

4. Quoted in K Knox, 'The Gulf War and Race Relations in Britain', *Patterns of Prejudice* 29 (1995), pp29-51.

5. Centre for Cultural Studies Race and Politics Group, *The Empire Strikes Back: Race and Racism in 70s Britain* (Hutchinson, London, 1982).

6. A Sivanandan, *A Different Hunger: Writings on Black Resistance* (Pluto Press, London, 1982) p109.

7. T Modood, 'The End of a Hegemony: The Concept of "Black" and British Asians', in J Rex & B Drury (eds), *Ethnic Mobilisation in a Multi-Cultural Europe* (Avebury, Aldershot, 1994), pp87-96.

8. T H Marshall, *Class, Citizenship and Social Development* (Anchor Books, New York, 1965), pp101-2.

9. W Kymlicka, *Multicultural Citizenship* (Oxford University Press, Oxford, 1995), p180.

2 HISTORICAL PERSPECTIVES

Britain has long been a country of immigration. Indeed, it is argued that, 'The British are clearly amongst the most ethnically composite of the Europeans'.[1] In the nineteenth century people from Ireland, Italy, Poland, Lithuania, Germany, France and many other countries emigrated to Britain. There was also substantial immigration by Jews fleeing persecution in eastern Europe. Major seaports, such as Liverpool, London and Cardiff, contained quite long established, though small, black communities. Immigration has continued in the twentieth century. In the inter-war period immigrants were often viewed negatively and discrimination was rife. Levels of immigration, and its perceived social effects, led to anti-immigrant political mobilisation. One consequence of this was a tightening of British immigration control. There are important lessons to be drawn from past political responses to 'problems' of immigration. This chapter begins by examining the experience of Irish and Jewish immigrants, before moving to explore aspects of the legacy of Empire. It ends by surveying the effects that pseudo-scientific theories of racial difference had on the politics of late nineteenth and early twentieth century Britain and Europe.

THE 'SPECIAL CASE' OF THE IRISH

In the nineteenth century the major immigrant group to Britain was Irish. Hundreds of thousands of Irish people emigrated, although Britain was by no means the only receiving country. Indeed, between 1874 and 1921, 84 per cent of people leaving Ireland chose to make a new life for themselves in the USA. Only 8 per cent came to Britain. Irish immigration to Britain was at its peak in the mid-nineteenth century. Table 2.1 shows its extent then.

Table 2.1 Irish immigration to Britain, 1841-71

Year	Settlers in England and Wales	Settlers in Scotland	Total
1841	289 404	126 321	415 725
1851	519 959	207 367	727 326
1861	601 634	204 083	805 717
1871	566 540	207 770	774 310

Source Census returns

At the start of the twentieth century Irish immigration to Britain declined. According to the 1901 Census, there were 426 565 Irish people in England and Wales and 205 064 in Scotland. By 1911 the numbers had fallen to 375 325 in England and Wales and 174 714 in Scotland. However, these figures underestimate the Irish population to Britain because in both cases the key census question focused on birthplace. For this reason neither census identified children born in Britain to Irish immigrants who continued to view themselves as Irish.

Some early migration was a consequence of religious tension between Catholics and Protestants. Some migration was seasonal as Irish people moved to Britain to seek harvesting work. Migration accelerated during the nineteenth century for two main reasons. The first was the severe economic hardship brought about by the potato famine, which began in 1845 and illustrated an important aspect of British colonial exploitation of the Irish economy. During the famine (or 'the starvation' as some have argued it might more accurately be called) the Irish economy continued to export food while Irish people went hungry. The second main reason was the demand for labour from the rapidly industrialising British economy, which lured Irish workers to British factories. This movement began to acquire the characteristics of a chain migration as other Irish people sought to join family and friends who had moved to Britain.

Irish people settled mainly in urban areas, and distinct Irish communities were established in cities such as Glasgow, Liverpool and Manchester. In these cities Irish people suffered many of the social problems that afflicted the poorest members of the working class during industrialisation. Such problems were worsened for the many Irish who left comparative rural tranquillity for an apartment in an overcrowded urban area. In their new communities the Irish sought to maintain their distinct culture, the Catholic church being central to many community activities. The concentration of Irish communities and their Catholicism provoked hostility on the part of the native population. Whether or not the discrimination experienced by Irish people can be categorised as racist has been an important area of debate.

It is clear that degrading Irish stereotypes – of laziness and fecklessness – were quite common, as was anti-Catholicism. Irish people were often victims of violent attack because of cultural distinctness. The discrimination was, though, not based on phenotypical differences of skin colour, meaning that anti-Irish discrimination differs from the experience of Asian and Afro-Caribbean immigrants in this important respect. Nevertheless, it is possible to argue that perceptions of Irish people as socially, culturally and economically inferior were racist. Whether or not this is the case, the ways in which anti-Irish stereotypes were constructed and acted upon provides us with an important perspective on hostility to post-war black immigrants.

On the part of policy makers, Ireland has always been viewed as a special case because Irish people were in the nineteenth century, and still are, free to move to and settle in Britain. Once resident, they are also entitled to vote. The origin of this relationship is the Act of Union 1800 which formally incorporated Ireland into the United Kingdom and turned Irish people into citizens of the UK. Neither independence in 1922, nor Ireland's exit from the Commonwealth in 1947, altered the free movement provisions established at the start of the nineteenth century. This was partly because it was considered much too difficult to control movement of people from Ireland. When legislation was introduced from 1962 onwards to control many forms of immigration, it did not apply to the Irish. Although the Commonwealth Immigrants Act 1962 did provide the home secretary of the day with reserve powers to control Irish immigration, these have never been exercised.

JEWISH IMMIGRATION

Britain also has a long history of Jewish settlement, as well as incidences of anti-Semitism. In 1290 Edward I expelled the Jews from England and it was not until the seventeenth century that Jewish people returned in any great numbers to Britain. Jewish immigration increased rapidly at the end of the nineteenth century. It has been estimated that between 1870 and 1914 120 000 Jews entered Britain, creating a total population of about 300 000 by the start of the first world war.

The main reason for increased Jewish immigration was persecution in eastern Europe. In Russia, for example, attempts to modernise and westernise the economy led 'conservative' elements opposed to reform to target Jews, who were seen as too western and capitalist. Jews were in a no-win situation because if they defended themselves they only confirmed, in the eyes of their attackers, their disloyalty to Russia. Many Jews believed that Britain would provide a safe haven.

At that time Britain concerned itself more with registration of what were called aliens than it did with control of immigration.

Many Jews settled in urban areas where housing was cheap, as more recent immigrants have also done. There were large Jewish communities in areas such as the East End of London and the Cheetham Hill district of Manchester. Many social problems brought about by rapid industrialisation and urbanisation, such as poor housing, overcrowding, bad sanitation and unemployment, disproportionately affected Jewish immigrants.

Some, though, laid responsibility for the socio-economic problems caused by industrialisation and urbanisation at the door of the immigrants themselves. Immigrants are often used as scapegoats when times are bad. The 1890s were perceived as years of national decline, marked by relatively high unemployment. For anti-immigration groups such as the British Brothers' League and the Immigration Reform Association, immigrants were the problem and the best way to solve it was to stop immigration. This short-sighted, nationalistic and racist articulation of the problem is revealed by some of the slogans used at the time (and since), such as 'England for the English'.

Anti-immigrant groups, which included racists and anti-Semites, were keen to portray Jews as a drain on social resources. This is another familiar refrain of the extreme right. In fact, the notion that immigrants were a drain on resources was spurious. In 1905 an average of 15.2 out of every 1000 members of the non-immigrant population were in the workhouse, compared to 1.7 out of every 1000 immigrants.[2] Rather paradoxically, anti-Semites also claimed to unearth a 'Jewish conspiracy' within the upper echelons of international finance and capital. The bogus *Protocols of the Elders of Zion* purported to map the collusion.

Groups such as the British Brothers' League, which was established in 1901 and had a membership of 45 000 in 1903, and the Immigration Reform Association had an important effect on the climate of opinion that influenced the Conservative government to bring forward legislation to control immigration. These groups managed to forge an unlikely alliance between Conservative MPs and workers from the East End of London. Patterns of settlement and the problematisation of issues of urban decay as immigrant-related help to explain aspects of the debate which culminated in the Aliens Act 1905.

TOWARDS IMMIGRATION CONTROL

In 1905 Arthur Balfour's Conservative government introduced the Aliens Order which applied to all non-UK subjects and sought to exclude 'undesirable and destitute aliens'. It contained three main provisions:

- power to refuse entry to immigrants without means of subsistence
- possible expulsion of aliens after one year if they were found to be receiving poor relief, found guilty of vagrancy or found to be living in insanitary and overcrowded conditions
- a guarantee that immigrants who would be subject to political or religious persecution in their country of origin would not be refused entry to Britain.

When the Liberals formed a government in 1906, they did not repeal the legislation, but, equally, they did not seek to enforce it in a restrictive way.

Following the outbreak of the first world war, the Aliens Restriction Act 1914 was passed, giving the government sweeping powers to control immigration. Two days after this Act was passed, the British Nationality and Status of Aliens Act 1914 gave the police and military authorities wide-ranging powers to inter or deport enemy aliens.

The end of the war did not see the removal of restrictive aliens legislation. In fact, further controls were introduced because of hostility to the defeated enemy and continued anti-Semitism. In addition, in 1919 there were violent racist attacks on black people in cities such as Liverpool and Cardiff. One reason for the attacks was high levels of unemployment among soldiers returning from the front. As has often happened, ethnic minorities served as convenient scapegoats for deeper social problems.

The Aliens Restriction (Amendment) Act 1919 extended the 1914 legislation for a further year, and was in fact renewed on an annual basis until it was replaced by the British Nationality Act 1981. In 1920 a new Aliens Order was introduced and gave immigration officers power to refuse entry to people who could not support themselves. If an immigrant wished to work in Britain he or she needed a permit issued to a prospective employer by the Ministry of Labour. Aliens were also required to register with the police.

Immigration officers also tried to bring people from long-established black communities within the purview of the legislation, thereby generating increased powers of deportation. It has been argued that as early as 1919 the 'liberal procedures of the Victorian age and indeed of the years between 1905 and 1914 belonged to a different and vanished world'.[3]

IMMIGRATION BETWEEN THE WARS

During the inter-war period continued movement of Jewish people took place. In the 1930s many fled the horrors of Nazi rule in Germany, Austria and Czechoslovakia. Between 1933 and the Nuremberg Laws of 1935, the Nazi regime stripped Jews of German nationality. About 50 000 Jewish people entered Britain between 1933 and 1939. Unlike their late nineteenth century counterparts from eastern Europe, many of these immigrants were educated and well-to-do.

Anti-Semites were not interested in such distinctions. From about 1934, Oswald Mosley's British Union of Fascists (BUF) developed a keen interest in the 'Jewish question', inspired by Hitler's Germany and the increased number of Jewish refugees arriving in Britain. The BUF was involved in a number of attacks on Jews in the East End of London, culminating in the 1936 'battle of Cable Street' which prompted introduction of the Public Order Act 1937. The BUF also stigmatised other immigrant groups, such as the Irish, for the very high levels of unemployment experienced in Britain during the great depression of the inter-war years.

Between the wars Jews began to move away from their original areas of settlement. In London, for example, they increasingly moved to the northern suburbs of Redbridge, Finchley and Barnet. In Manchester there was similar movement from inner-city Cheetham Hill to the leafier environs of Prestwich. It has been argued that these refugees from Nazism made a substantial contribution to the British economy. Jewish and non-Jewish refugees from Nazism created several times more new jobs than there were numbers of immigrants.[4]

In the inter-war years Jews also became more prominent in political life. Initial political activity took place within the Labour Party, reflecting patterns of settlement, traditions of support for the left and socio-economic status. The increased number of Jews on the Conservative benches in the House of Commons and in the cabinet in the 1980s indicates upward social mobility and a change in political allegiance.

The largest immigrant and immigrant-origin group in Britain between the wars continued to be the Irish. In 1921 the number of Irish-born people in England and Wales was 364 747 (1 per cent of the total population). By 1931 it had increased to 381 089 (still 1 per cent). In Scotland the same years witnessed a fall in numbers from 159 020 (3.3 per cent) to 124 296 (2.6 per cent). After the first world war Britain became the main destination of Irish immigrants. One reason for this was the introduction of immigration control legislation in the USA between 1921 and the Johnson-Reed Act passed in 1924.

Despite some evidence of upward social mobility, the Irish continued to be concentrated in the lower socio-economic groupings, and Irish communities were to be found in areas of towns and cities where the effects of urban decay were disproportionately felt. Irish people were often employed in heavy industry, railway and road construction and in types of employment that British workers were unwilling to do.

The black population in Britain remained small despite tough economic conditions in the Caribbean and freedom for colonial subjects to enter Britain. They were deterred from doing so by high levels of British unemployment during the depression, and by reports throughout the Empire of racist attacks in Britain, such as those which took place in 1919.

Some superficial evidence pointed to greater acceptance of black people. Paul Robeson took the lead in *Othello* in 1930 and West Indian cricket star Learie Constantine was a big success playing league cricket in Lancashire in the 1920s. However, Robeson was refused admission to a party held in his honour at the Savoy Grill, and scandalised public opinion when he kissed his co-star, Peggy Ashcroft. Constantine wrote of the discrimination he faced in his book *The Colour Bar*.

The position of members of Britain's black communities became more precarious as official hostility increased. The Special Restriction (Coloured Seamen) Act 1925 placed the burden of proof of British citizenship on black people, whereas it had previously been assumed that they were British. Rigorous enforcement of this legislation during the 1930s consigned almost all black men to unemployment.

In response, the black population began to mobilise politically between the wars. One prominent group was the League of Coloured Peoples, established in 1931 by a doctor of Jamaican origin, Harold Moody. The League sought to chart a middle course between radical black organisations, such as the West African Students' Union, and paternalistic, often white-led associations. It took as its slogan not 'Black against White' but 'Black with White'.

THE LEGACY OF EMPIRE

By the end of the nineteenth century Britain was a major colonial power. It was outward looking, economically powerful and colonising. Also, during the nineteenth century social thinkers began to pay closer attention to the effects of alleged racial differences on social ordering. Slavery had only been abolished in Britain in 1807 and had left behind it an important legacy of racist attitudes. The experience of Empire and the development of pseudo-scientific ideas of supposed racial difference played important parts in the development of racism in Britain.

Powerful economic and political imperatives underpinned colonisation. It allowed exploitation of natural resources in colonies and provided markets for products from Britain's industrialised economy. Britain's imperial expansion also gave it additional clout in international power politics. Britain colonised extensively in Africa, Asia and the Caribbean.

The British, though, sought justifications other than economic for colonisation. It was argued that colonised cultures were inferior and in need of modernisation, thereby creating what Rudyard Kipling called 'the white man's burden'. This fostered a paternalistic relationship between colonised and coloniser, with colonised cultures viewed as inferior. In addition, as independence movements became more prominent throughout the colonies the form of stereotyping changed. Following the Indian mutiny of 1857, Indians were increasingly portrayed as 'deceptive, fanatical and cruel'.[5]

Attitudes became increasingly hostile towards the end of the nineteenth century as pseudo-scientific notions of racial difference came to greater prominence. When colonial subjects moved to Britain they entered a society where stereotypes based on alleged racial and cultural inferiority 'which instantly relegated non-whites to an inferior status and rank' had already developed.[6]

Towards the end of the nineteenth century there was increased interest in 'scientific' theories of race and social structure. These were inspired to some extent by the work of Charles Darwin on the origin of species and the process of evolution. Darwin's theory of evolution proved that Europeans were related to Africans and human beings were related to apes. His ideas were, however, applied by some social thinkers to human beings and, on the basis of a misinterpretation, it was argued that there was a racial ordering among humans. This led to social Darwinism, the advocates of which contended that human life was analogous to Darwin's idea of the survival of the fittest. Colonisation and subjugation could be legitimised on these grounds.

Darwin's cousin, Francis Galton, president of the British Anthropological Association between 1885 and 1889, used techniques of anthropometry to measure human skeletons as a way of illustrating the diversity of human races and the supposed superiority of white Anglo-Saxons. Another book entitled *The Living Races of Mankind* pointed to the 'muscular development' of black people and their lower pain threshold which the authors claimed meant that operations could be conducted on them without anaesthetic.

The notion of racial ordering was also implicit in remarks made by British prime minister Benjamin Disraeli who, in what can be seen as a justification of British imperialism, remarked to a parliamentary colleague in 1849 that, 'Race implies difference and difference implies superiority, and superiority leads to predominance'.[7] Even during the nineteenth century when, as we have seen, black communities in Britain were small, ideas of racial superiority and inferiority were influenced both by Empire and the pseudo-scientific notions of racial difference that justified colonisation.

In other European countries, pseudo-scientific theories of racial difference had major effects. Nazi 'philosophers' identified a Euro-Aryan civilisation and a 'master race'. They also rejected the liberal principles of the Enlightenment – with its emphasis on individual rights – and focused on the collective destiny of peoples distinguished by 'blood ties'. The 'revolt against reason' contained within these ideas of racial difference underpinned the Nazi ideology which disfigured the twentieth century.

Historians have analysed the impact of Empire on British racism. From a radical perspective Fryer points to development of racist ideologies in nineteenth-century Britain and ways in which they could be used to justify the actions of the ruling class:

> Could racism now be dispensed with? By no means. It was too valuable. A new basis and purpose for it had emerged. It was to become a principal hand-maiden to Empire. The culminating stage in the rise of English racism was the development of a strident pseudo-scientific mythology of race that would become the most important ingredient in British imperial history.[8]

Rich argues that Fryer is too 'fatalistic' and that British 'middle opinion', by which he means the central body of informed thought, 'acted as a cushion against the more general extension of systematic racist doctrines in the nineteenth and twentieth centuries'. He further claims that 'cultural provincialism' affected attitudes to immigrants after the second world war. It is Rich's view that, 'The English Channel acted as a crucial ideological and intellectual barrier on matters of race well into the twentieth century'.[9]

IMMIGRATION AND THE BRITISH

Britain has a long history of immigration and, like any other dynamic society, has been shaped by movements of people both into and out of it, as well as within its borders. Industrialisation, urbanisation and Empire all played prominent parts in the development of British racism. Responses to immigration in the nineteenth and early twentieth century are of intrinsic interest to students of British history. They also yield valuable insights in analysis of more recent developments.

First, it is possible to identify similarities in patterns of settlement. Immigrants usually start life in Britain at the bottom of the socio-economic pile. This means that their access to employment and housing opportunities is limited. For these reasons, large immigrant communities developed in many British cities at the end of the nineteenth century. Problems of inner-city life, such as poor housing, overcrowding, bad sanitation and unemployment, quickly became 'problems of immigration'. Distinct parallels can be drawn between the hostility shown towards Jews in the East End of London around a century (and less) ago, and more recent manifestations of racism directed at the large Bangladeshi community resident in what is now Tower Hamlets.

Second, political mobilisation has taken place in response to the 'threat' and 'problem' of immigration. In the past groups such as the British Brothers' League and the BUF espoused a racist and nationalistic problematisation of the issue of immigration, and argued that the cure for social problems was an end to immigration. The racist 'quick fix' is also an important part of the platform of more recent anti-immigrant groups, such as the National Front (NF) and the British National Party.

Third, anti-immigrant political mobilisation has played a part in the development of immigration control policies adopted by mainstream parties. Mainstream politicians may eschew the more overt anti-Semitism and racism of the extreme right, but they have responded to the fears that such groups play upon by enacting legislation which accepts the potentially racist and nationalistic logic of anti-immigrant arguments. This runs as follows: immigration is at the heart of many problems of perceived urban and social decay, thus immigrants are the problem, therefore legislation to restrict immigration will go some way to solving the problem (as defined). Parallels can be drawn between the climate of opinion preceding early twentieth century immigration control and formulation of the race relations policy paradigm in the 1960s.

Finally, notions of racial and cultural superiority and inferiority, bolstered by pseudo-scientific ideas of racial hierarchies, have served to justify colonisation (just as they were used to defend slavery). Even when there was not a large black presence in Britain notions of racial difference entered into aspects of everyday life and were articulated as 'common sense' racism based on notions of superiority and inferiority that are fundamentally misconceived but hard to tackle.

It is in the historical context presented in this chapter that the social demography of multi-ethnic Britain needs to be assessed. In the next chapter the socio-economic profile of Britain's ethnic minorities is examined in detail.

NOTES

1. J Geipel, *The Europeans: An Ethnohistorical Survey* (Longman, Harlow, 1969), pp163-4.
2. J Walvin, *Passage to Britain* (Penguin, Harmondsworth, 1984), p65.
3. C Holmes, *John Bull's Island: Immigration and British Society 1871-1971* (Macmillan, London, 1988), p114.
4. Ibid, p128.
5. R Miles, *Racism* (Routledge, London, 1989), p83.
5. Walvin, op cit, p44.
7. Walvin, op cit, p40.
8. P Fryer, *Staying Power: The History of Black People in Britain* (Pluto Press, London, 1984), p165.
9. P Rich, *Race and Empire in British Politics* (Cambridge University Press, Cambridge, 1986), p5.

3 THE NUMBERS GAME

Numbers are an important aspect of the politics of immigration and race. On the one hand, they may be misused by populist politicians to exploit the 'threat' of immigration. In the 1960s, anti-immigration groups focused on numbers of New Commonwealth immigrants in their definition of the immigration problem. If the 'problem' was numbers of New Commonwealth immigrants, then the 'solution' was restriction. On the other hand, statistical sources can play a part in tackling discrimination, as collation of accurate data on exclusion can support strategies designed to achieve greater equality. This is one reason why, for the first time, the 1991 Census asked respondents about ethnic origin. In this chapter some features of post-war immigration are explored through investigation of the 1991 Census and other statistical sources. These sources throw light on many aspects of multi-ethnic Britain's social demography. Areas of settlement, socio-economic status, (un)employment, education and housing are all examined. These statistical sources show, among other things, the importance of refining the terms 'black' and 'ethnic minority' to take account of differing patterns of success and exclusion.

THE 1991 CENSUS

Since 1841, every census of the UK population has contained a question on country of birth. In 1971 a question which asked respondents about their parents' country of birth was added. However, this was an unsatisfactory way of assessing ethnic origin, because many Asian people entered Britain from East African countries such as Uganda and Kenya. The question could not therefore accurately capture ethnic origin. For this reason, the 1991 Census asked respondents a question about ethnic origin.

A question of this kind was in fact proposed for the 1981 Census. However, when tests for the census were undertaken in 1979 a degree of opposition emerged. In the Haringey area of London, which has a large black population, the question received a poor set of responses. Furthermore, some were concerned about the use to which ethnic origin data would be put. Would it be used to combat racism, or to advance the arguments of the anti-immigration/immigrant lobby? Some feared that the latter was more likely. For these reasons, the question was not included in the 1981 Census.

Nevertheless, in 1983 the House of Commons home affairs sub-committee on race relations and immigration recommended inclusion of a question on ethnic origin in the 1991 Census. The 1991 Census white paper, published in 1988, also proposed inclusion of an ethnic origin question. When the 1989 test generated a positive response, the decision was taken to incorporate the question.[1]

The 1991 Census ethnic origin question gave respondents nine categories to choose from: White, Black-Caribbean, Black-African, Black-Other, Indian, Pakistani, Bangladeshi, Chinese and Any Other Ethnic Group. The two categories Black-Other and Any Other Ethnic Group were included to allow individuals to describe their own ethnic group if they felt none of the other categories to be suitable. The Census Offices developed a classification system with 35 categories: the seven pre-set answers and 28 categories based on respondents' own written-in answer. In the following analysis these Census categories are mainly used.

The 1991 Census showed that previous surveys which had sought to gauge the size of various ethnic groups, such as the Labour Force Survey (LFS), had in fact underestimated the size of Britain's ethnic minority population. The pooled 1988-90 LFS data put the total ethnic minority population at 4.9 per cent of the total UK population. Pooled data were thought to be the most reliable way of interpreting LFS data because it uses population samples. Even within the LFS's quite large samples people from ethnic minorities were a relatively small group. Putting the three data sets together was seen as a good way of increasing accuracy.

However, the more reliable 1991 Census's ethnic origin question showed the total ethnic minority population to be 5.5 per cent of the UK population, 11 per cent more than the estimate generated from LFS data. LFS underestimation was linked to higher levels of non-participation amongst ethnic minorities and a greater reluctance to answer the LFS ethnic group question.

Table 3.1 Resident population by ethnic group, 1991

Ethnic group	Number ('000s)	% of total pop	% of the pop of Other groups
All groups	54 889	100.0	–
White	51 874	94.5	–
Other groups	3 015	5.5	100.0
Black Caribbean	500	0.9	16.6
Black African	212	0.4	7.0
Black Other	178	0.3	5.9
Black total	891	1.6	29.5
Indian	840	1.5	27.9
Pakistani	477	0.9	15.8
Bangladeshi	163	0.3	5.4
Chinese	157	0.3	5.2
Other groups – Asian	198	0.4	6.6
Other (non-Asian)	290	0.5	9.6

Source 1991 Census

The Census returns (Table 3.1) revealed that 94.5 per cent of the UK population identified themselves as belonging to the White ethnic group. Just over three million people, or 5.5 per cent of the population, described themselves as belonging to an ethnic group other than White. The largest ethnic group was Indians, who comprised 1.5 per cent of the total UK population and 27.9 per cent of the UK's ethnic minority population.

Two of the categories used by the Census were felt by some to be misleading. These people argued that the Black-Other and Black-Caribbean categories should be combined to give a clear indication of the population of Afro-Caribbean origin, because close analysis of the figures showed a big dip in the Black-Caribbean population in the 0-19 age cohort. This dip cannot be explained simply by normal rates of population growth. A more plausible explanation is that parents of Caribbean origin ticked the box Black-Other for their children and wrote British in the additional information section.[2] An accurate figure for the British population of Caribbean origin – combining the categories Black-Caribbean and Black-Other – is thus about 678 000 (1.2 per cent).

Table 3.2 shows regional distribution of the ethnic minority population in 1991. It was disproportionately concentrated in metropolitan areas (78 per cent compared to 42 per cent of the white population). More than half lived in the southeast, compared with less than a third (31 per cent) of the total population. The largest population concentration was in Greater London, where 44.6 per cent of people from ethnic minorities resided, compared with 10.3 per cent of the white population. There were substantial Asian communities in the Midlands and the North. The largest Indian community in Britain was found to be in Leicester, while the largest Pakistani community was in Bradford.

Table 3.2 Regional distribution of population by ethnic group, 1991

Area	Total %	White %	Ethnic minorities %
Britain	100.0	100.0	100.0
England and Wales	90.9	90.5	97.9
England	85.7	85.1	96.5
North	5.5	5.8	1.3
Yorkshire	8.8	8.9	7.1
East Midlands	7.2	7.3	6.2
East Anglia	3.7	3.8	1.4
Southeast	31.4	29.9	56.2
Greater London	12.2	10.3	44.6
Southwest	8.4	8.8	2.1
West Midlands	9.4	9.1	14.1
Northwest	11.4	11.6	8.1
Wales	5.2	5.4	1.4
Scotland	9.1	9.5	2.1
All Met districts (England)	42.0	39.9	78.0
Excluding London	29.8	29.6	33.4
All non-Met districts	58.0	60.1	22.0

Source 1991 Census

Ethnic minorities are disproportionately represented in the younger age cohorts, particularly people of Pakistani and Bangladeshi origin. It has been calculated, on the basis of zero net immigration, that the ethnic minority population will eventually stabilise at about 9 per cent of the total.[3] This young age profile has clear implications for education, employment and other policy.

CLASS

The 1991 Census permits analysis of the socio-economic status of ethnic minorities. Many immigrants started life in Britain at the bottom of the socio-economic pile doing poorly-paid jobs. Table 3.3 suggests that ethnic minority groups have, in general, failed to attain parity with the white population. Nevertheless, against that background we see some evidence of upward social mobility. Indians, for example, were almost twice as likely as white people to be occupied in the professions. This has led to talk of a 'new Indian middle class'.[4]

Pakistanis were less upwardly mobile but also slightly exceed the norm for occupation in the professions. They were under-represented as managers and technicians and over-represented as skilled/manual workers. There were also differences within the Asian population as in socio-economic terms Bangladeshis fell well behind people of Indian or Pakistani origin and were over-represented in semi-skilled and skilled manual occupations. There was also a greater than average concentration of ethnic minority men and women in the public sector and a higher than average level of self-employment among Indian, Pakistani and Bangladeshi men and women, for example in the retail sector and restaurant trade.

Table 3.3 Socio-economic status by selected ethnic group, 1991

Occupation	White	Indians	Pakistanis	Bangladeshis	Black-Caribbean
	%	%	%	%	%
Unskilled	6	3	5	4	7
Semi-skilled	15	21	24	32	19
Skilled manual	21	16	25	26	22
Skilled non-manual	24	23	18	20	24
Managerial	29	28	22	13	26
Professional	5	9	6	5	2

Source 1991 Census

The amalgamated Census categories Black-Caribbean and Black-Other were under-represented in professional and managerial occupations and over-represented in semi-skilled and skilled manual occupations. Black-Africans, on the other hand, were above the norm at both the top and bottom of the socio-economic pile in the professions and in unskilled occupations (Table 3.3).

UNEMPLOYMENT

In addition to analysis of people in work, the census permits assessment of unemployment levels. Table 3.4 presents levels of unemployment among ethnic minorities. Table 3.5 complements it by presenting earnings levels.

Table 3.4 Unemployment by sex and ethnic group, 1994

Sex	All origins	White	All ethnic minorities	Black	Indian	Pakistani/ Bangladeshi
	%	%	%	%	%	%
Men	10.4	9.9	21.4	30	13	27
Women	7.0	6.6	15.3	19	11	26
All	8.9	8.4	18.8	25	12	26

Source Labour Force Survey 1994

Table 3.5 Average hourly earnings by sex and ethnic group, 1994

Sex	All origins	White	All ethnic minorities	Black	Indian	Pakistani/ Bangladeshi
	£	£	£	£	£	£
Men	7.97	8.0	7.15	7.03	7.29	5.47
Women	6.39	6.40	6.31	6.77	5.77	5.15
All	7.42	7.44	6.82	6.92	6.70	5.39

Source Labour Force Survey 1994

Recent LFS data has been revised to take account of Census information on the ethnic minority population. The LFS also merges the Census's black categories. In 1994 it found unemployment rates among ethnic minorities to be double those for white people.[5] The highest rates were among black people and those of Pakistani and Bangladeshi origin. People of Indian origin were only slightly more likely to be unemployed than white people.

The LFS also shows average hourly earnings for ethnic minority employees working full-time to be about 92 per cent of those of white employees. Women from ethnic minorities earned roughly the same as white women (and less than men). Men from ethnic minorities earned about 89 per cent of the earnings of white men.

EDUCATION

Education and training are closely linked to employment issues. In particular, lower labour market participation rates among ethnic minorities in the 16-19 age cohort are linked to higher rates of participation in further and higher education.

Table 3.6 shows significantly higher than average participation in education by 16- to 19-year-olds from ethnic minorities. Young people of Caribbean and Bangladeshi origin are only slightly above the norm. Africans, Chinese, African Asians, Indians and Pakistanis are much higher. This could be because young people from ethnic minorities are more motivated. They may also receive better parental support as educational attainment may be more highly valued. It may also reflect failings of the state school system which have to be made good through further education. Also, high levels of unemployment may 'encourage' young people from ethnic minorities to stay in education as a way of enhancing their chances in the labour market.

Table 3.6 Percentage of 16- to 19-year-olds in full-time education by ethnic group, 1988-89

	All	Male	Female
All origins	39	38	40
White	37	36	38
Total ethnic minority	56	56	56
Afro-Caribbean	43	39	48
African Asian	66	75	56
Indian	58	55	61
Pakistani	55	64	45
Bangladeshi	46	41	*
Chinese	77	*	*
African	71	*	*
Other/mixed	58	55	62

Note An asterisk indicates sample size was too small

Source T Jones, *Britain's Ethnic Minorities* (Policy Studies Institute, London, 1993), p44

Levels of attainment are also important. Early studies tended to point to lower levels of attainment by pupils of Asian or Afro-Caribbean origin. However, recent studies have suggested that these patterns may not be as clear as first thought. There are, for example, marked differences in performance within the Asian population, as pupils of Indian origin perform better than those of Bangladeshi origin. However, social class and educational outcomes are themselves strongly related.[6] Given the evidence in Table 3.3, it is not particularly surprising that the more upwardly mobile population of Indian origin performs better at school than do pupils of Bangladeshi origin who are more likely to be working class.

The content of school curricula has also been a controversial issue. As Layton-Henry put it:

> How far can minority cultures, languages and values be recognised, respected and incorporated into national educational systems which place a high priority on transmitting a common core of beliefs and values such as patriotism and democracy? Will national cohesion be undermined if monocultural education gives way to multicultural education?[7]

In the 1980s anti-racist education developed in some parts of Britain, usually in Labour-controlled local authorities. Such policies were held to have backfired following the death in 1988 of an Asian pupil at Burnage High School in Manchester.

In 1995 it was suggested that pupils should be taught 'Britishness' as part of the national curriculum. Critics of this view soon pointed out the extreme difficulty of defining 'Britishness', and argued that in reality advocates of teaching national identity were social conservatives seeking to pursue assimilationist ideals.

HOUSING

In the 1950s immigrants faced widespread discrimination in the housing market. Access to housing was made difficult because of discrimination in the private housing sector and the public housing allocation process. Many immigrants were forced into the worst public housing stock or the private rented sector, where conditions were often appalling. It was not uncommon in the 1950s for landlords advertising vacancies to put up 'No Coloureds or Irish' signs. Anti-discrimination legislation in the 1960s ended this practice (or at least the notices came down).

As in the late nineteenth and early twentieth centuries, immigrants were made scapegoats for urban decay. Social problems became 'race problems'. One racist MP in the late 1950s even went so far as to suggest that immigrants preferred overcrowded conditions because it kept them warm and reminded them of home. In fact, many Asian immigrants preferred to buy their own homes, and a flourishing shadow Asian financial services market developed providing Asian people with mortgage finance denied by racist banks and building societies.

Table 3.7 Household tenure by selected ethnic group, 1991

Type	White	Indians	Pakistanis	Bangladeshis	Black-Caribbean
	%	%	%	%	%
Local authority	22	8	11	38	42
Housing association	3	2	2	6	11
Privately rented	7	7	10	10	18
Buying	43	66	57	41	25
Owned	25	17	20	5	3

Source 1991 Census

The 1991 Census revealed patterns of housing tenure. Table 3.7 shows that Indians and Pakistanis were above the population average for owner-occupation. This should not necessarily be seen as a sign of economic success or social mobility. In the 1950s and 1960s discrimination in the public and private housing sectors led many Asian people to purchase homes. They often bought run-down properties in the less desirable parts of towns. In addition, many Asians settled in towns in the Midlands and the North where property is cheaper. This was not the case for people from the Caribbean, who settled predominantly in London. Bangladeshis settled in areas of East London, such as Tower Hamlets, where property is expensive.

DISCRIMINATION

The LFS attributed high rates of ethnic minority unemployment to the younger age profile of the ethnic minority population, to lower levels of qualifications, and to regional and industrial distribution. These factors may play a part in explaining variance between ethnic groups. Many Pakistanis who settled in areas in the North and Midlands were attracted by the prospect of employment in the manufacturing industries that had traditionally been a mainstay of the economies of those areas. The recent decline of British manufacturing has hit such people particularly hard.

What the LFS does not mention is racism. There is evidence of exclusion in the labour market and in relative rates of pay. What is not clear is the extent to which racist attitudes contribute to this exclusion. Between 1974 and 1976 a detailed survey of racism in Britain was conducted, based on interviews with 3292 people of Asian or Afro-Caribbean origin. The survey found that Britain's two million black people 'show up in highly disproportionate terms in all unfavourable social statistics'.[8]

It is very difficult to conduct attitudinal surveys, such as opinion polls, into racism. Most people if asked whether or not they are racist will deny it. However, it has been argued that a way of bypassing this defensive reaction is to ask people whether they think 'the people on their street' are prejudiced. Individuals can then impute their prejudice onto the general public whilst steering clear of a personal admission of racism. Individuals may answer truthfully and say that they are not prejudiced but that people on their street are. However, this clearly cannot be true if everyone replies that they are not prejudiced but that people on their street are. As AG Bennett wittily put it:

> Since I come 'ere I never met a single English person who 'ad any colour prejudice. Once I walked the whole length of a street looking for a room, and everyone told me that he or she 'ad no prejudice against coloured people. It was the neighbour who was stupid. If we could only find the 'neighbour' we could solve the entire problem. But to find 'im is the trouble! Neighbours are the worst people to live beside in this country.[9]

A 1994 opinion poll asked white people how much prejudice they thought there was in Britain, how prejudiced they were and how prejudiced they thought people on their street were. The responses are shown in Tables 3.8 and 3.9. The questions were unsatisfactory in that they focus on black people – seen as people of African or Caribbean origin – and do not give information on prejudicial attitudes towards Asians. However, what the data show is that an overwhelming majority (79 per cent) of white people believe there to be widespread racism in Britain.

Table 3.8 Prejudice against black people in Britain, 1995

	Now	1991	1987	1983
A lot	40	50	57	50
A little	39	41	33	40
Hardly any	4	7	7	7
Don't know	7	3	2	3

Note Original question: How much prejudice is there in Britain against black people – that is, people whose families were originally from the West Indies or Africa?

Source ICM/The *Guardian*

Table 3.9 Assessments of own and neighbours' racial prejudice in Britain, 1995

	You yourself	People in your street
Very prejudiced	3	9
A little prejudiced	16	32
Not prejudiced at all	80	59

Note Original question: How prejudiced are you yourself against people of other races and how prejudiced are people in your street?

Source ICM/The *Guardian*

There is also a discrepancy in the poll between levels of people who claim not to be prejudiced at all (80 per cent) and levels of people on their street with a similar lack of prejudice (59 per cent). This suggests that some people may prefer not to admit to their discriminatory attitudes, preferring to impute them to others.

USING STATISTICS

Statistics such as those presented in this chapter need to be placed in their proper context as ways of explaining social reality in contemporary Britain. What they provide is merely a snapshot of some areas of modern life. Information on class, employment, education and housing gives insights into the effects of post-war immigration and racism on British society. However, while there is evidence of socio-economic inequality as well as exclusion in housing and (un)employment, it is difficult to generalise about 'blacks' or 'ethnic minorities' because patterns of exclusion are not uniform across all groups. Sweeping statements almost always belie a rather more complex social reality.

In addition, the ways in which issues of racist exclusion are cross-cut by factors such as class, region and gender generate further complexity. It is simply not possible to extract immigration and its effects from the class structure of British society. Immigrants and their descendants are disproportionately concentrated among the working classes. However, because of racism, their status is not analogous to that of the white working class. When analysing employment statistics, high levels of Pakistani and Bangladeshi unemployment are linked to settlement in regions that have experienced industrial decline. Also, gender divisions are strong in modern society. It is therefore no surprise to find perpetuation of these divisions within the ethnic minority population.

In the 1960s 'the numbers game' played a key part in the development of a policy framework which emphasised increasingly strict immigration control. The next chapter explores the origins and form of British race relations policy in the 1960s and 1970s. It looks in particular at factors which affected political debate on immigration and race, as a way of understanding how these issues became problematised.

NOTES

1. C Owen, 'Using the Labour Force Survey to Estimate Britain's Ethnic Minority Populations', *Population Trends* 72 (Summer 1993), pp18-27.
2. R Ballard and V Singh Kabra, *The Ethnic Dimensions of the 1991 Census: A Preliminary Report* (Census Dissemination Unit, University of Manchester, 1994).
3. Ibid, pp15-22.
4. V Robinson, 'Roots to Mobility: The Social Mobility of Britain's Black Population 1981-87', *Ethnic and Racial Studies* 13 (1990), pp274-86.
5. F Sly, 'Ethnic Groups and the Labour Market: Analyses from the Spring 1994 Labour Force Survey', *Employment Gazette*, June 1995, pp251-62.
6. D Mason, *Race and Ethnicity in Modern Britain* (Oxford University Press, Oxford, 1995), p68.
7. Z Layton-Henry, *The Politics of Immigration* (Blackwell, Oxford, 1992), p222.
8. D Smith, *Racial Disadvantage in Britain: The PEP Report* (Penguin, Harmondsworth, 1977), p13.
9. A G Bennett, quoted in Holmes, op cit, p209.

4 RACE RELATIONS

Legislation passed in 1962, 1968 and 1971 restricted immigration into the UK. Legislation passed in 1965, 1968 and 1976 sought to combat racism within the UK. This combination of measures – tightening controls and seeking integration of already-settled immigrants and their descendants – has been the principal characteristic of British race relations policy. To explain why policy developed in this way in the 1960s and 1970s it is necessary to understand the nature of the problem with which policy makers believed themselves to be faced. The immigration issue had in fact become 'racialised' by the late 1950s, meaning that it was conceived as a problem not simply of immigration but of 'coloured' immigration by people from New Commonwealth countries and Pakistan. Hostility to this immigration, including anti-immigrant riots, grew during the 1950s and early 1960s. From 1962 to 1971 legislation was put in place by both Conservative and Labour governments effectively to end primary immigration from the New Commonwealth and Pakistan. At the same time legislation, culminating in the Race Relations Act 1976, outlawed certain manifestations of racism. This chapter analyses the political debates underpinning development of the race relations paradigm. It looks at ways in which the two main parties sought to establish a bipartisan consensus to 'neutralise' the immigration issue, and at challenges, such as Enoch Powell's, to it.

TYPES OF MIGRATION

The principal motive for immigration into Britain after the second world war was economic. The British economy needed more workers than could be provided by indigenous labour. Immigrants sought a better life for themselves and their families. Migrant labour was an answer to labour shortages.

It was, though, not an entirely 'logical' answer, because black immigrants were viewed negatively by existing UK residents, despite holding British passports and being entitled to come to the UK. Notions of 'racial purity' played a part in this lack of enthusiasm about what was called 'coloured' immigration. In 1949 the Royal Commission on

Population recognised the need for immigration but preferred immigrants 'of good human stock... not prevented by their religion or race from intermarrying with the host population and becoming merged into it.'

The principal characteristic of economically motivated immigration – known as primary migration – was that it was male-dominated. Areas of settlement were determined by availability of work. This generated large immigrant populations in London, the industrial towns of the Midlands – such as Birmingham, Coventry and Wolverhampton – and in northern mill towns – such as Bolton, Bradford and Oldham. Immigrant communities tended to be concentrated in particular areas of these towns and cities.

The period between 1948 and 1962 has been seen as a period of free entry into Britain for citizens from the former Empire and newly-emerging Commonwealth. However, scrutiny of cabinet papers reveals elite disquiet about the consequences of black immigration. Research has shown that the Conservative government seriously contemplated immigration controls in 1955.[1] In fact, the Conservatives had already drawn up immigration control legislation by 1954, but did not introduce it.

Primary migration was supplemented by family reunification, known as secondary migration. An important feature of secondary migration was the large number of women who came to Britain to join their husbands. The arrival of families consolidated and gave a greater air of permanence to immigrant communities. It helped end 'the myth of return' that immigrants would one day return to their country of origin. This became less likely as immigrants became more settled in Britain in the 1960s and 1970s. It is now even less so as second and third generation Britons of immigrant origin often know relatively little of their parents' or grandparents' countries of origin.

During the 1960s immigration controls were introduced and primary migration was effectively ended by the Immigration Act 1971. During the 1970s secondary migration continued, but gradually decreased. Governments have progressively sought to tighten rules on family reunification. For some years, one way this was done was the notorious, and now outlawed, virginity test for Asian women entering Britain for purposes of marriage.

In the 1960s and 1970s there was also movement to Britain by Asians from East African countries. This was caused by the 'Africanisation' policies pursued by governments in Kenya (1967-68), Uganda (1972-73) and Malawi (1976). It serves as an example of the third type of immigration into Britain, political refugees and asylum seekers, although East African Asians in fact held British passports.

POST-WAR IMMIGRATION

Immigrants did not only come from former colonies. Some came from Europe under the government-initiated European Volunteer Workers (EVW) programme. This programme committed the British government to meet the recruitment and transport costs of about 85 000 EVWs for employment in industries in which labour shortages were particularly acute. Many EVWs were refugees fleeing Soviet or Communist rule in countries such as Lithuania, Latvia, Estonia, Poland and Yugoslavia. By 1948 the scheme had cost £2.75 million.

The advantage of the EVW scheme was that its contracted labour was relatively malleable. The workers could be deployed wherever the needs of capital were greatest. The government also saw EVWs as more 'racially compatible' with the existing UK population than the initially small number of black immigrants who entered Britain from former colonies.

It is also important to note that the largest single immigrant group to enter Britain between 1946 and 1962 was still the Irish (Table 4.1), as had been the case since the mid-nineteenth century. It was, though, New Commonwealth immigration which was seen as particularly problematic, not immigration per se. Even so, other immigrant groups, such as Polish miners in Yorkshire, were subjected to prejudice and discrimination.

The chronological pattern of settlement by New Commonwealth immigrants passed through a series of distinct phases (Table 4.2). During the 1960s immigration from Asian countries such as India and Pakistan began to exceed that from the Caribbean. Most immigrants from the Caribbean came from Jamaica. Most Indian immigrants in the 1950s were Sikhs from eastern Punjab, while the majority of Muslims came from Mirpur and Sylhet in Pakistan. Beyond their Muslim faith there was little that these two groups had in common, although white people were – and remain – generally unaware of such differences.

Table 4.1 Estimated total net immigration from the Commonwealth and Ireland into the UK, 1946-62

Country	Number	Percentage
Australia	80 850	7.5
Canada	18 000	1.7
Central African Federation	5600	0.5
Ceylon	6300	0.6
Cyprus	33 400	3.1
East Africa	8900	0.8
India & Pakistan	150 900	14.0
Malaya	8100	0.7
Malta	16 400	1.5
New Zealand	23 400	2.2
West Africa	20 400	1.9
West Indies	263 700	24.4
Other Commonwealth	23 300	2.1
Total Commonwealth	659 250	61.0
Republic of Ireland	421 850	39.0

Source *Studies on Immigration from the Commonwealth* (Economist Intelligence Unit, London, 1963)

Table 4.2 Year of entry of ethnic minority populations born outside the UK

	Total ethnic minority immigrants	Afro-Caribbean	African	Indian	Pakistani	Bangladeshi
pre-1950	1	3	0	2	0	1
1951-60	11	36	1	10	6	5
1961-70	33	48	30	42	35	15
1971-80	32	8	55	32	35	32
1981-90	22	5	14	15	23	48

Source T Jones, *Britain's Ethnic Minorities* (Policy Studies Institute, London, 1993), p25

THE PRE-POLITICAL CONSENSUS

Historian Peter Fryer has described the period between 1958 and 1968 as one of a 'surrender to racism': 'Between 1958 and 1968 black

settlers in Britain watched the racist tail wag the parliamentary dog...
step by step racism was institutionalised, legitimised and nation-
alised'.[2] This claim sits uneasily alongside evidence that the Conservative government was considering immigration control legislation in
the mid-1950s. Successive legislation effectively ended primary immigration from New Commonwealth countries. Prior to introduction of
the 1962 Commonwealth Immigrants Bill pressure grew on the Conservative government to introduce legislation to restrict New Commonwealth immigration. This pressure came from a number of sources.

One was increased hostility towards immigrants. In August and
September 1958 in Nottingham and Notting Hill there were anti-
immigrant disturbances. In Notting Hill 'teddy boys' attacked West
Indians, Africans and Asians. In the wake of attacks on immigrants in
Nottingham the town's two MPs – one Conservative and one Labour
– called for an end to black immigration and for new deportation
laws. Immigrants were made scapegoats for what were in reality
attacks on them, as other MPs pointed out.

In a similar fashion, immigration and immigrants were linked to social
and urban problems such as poor housing, poverty, crime, vice and
disease. Immigrants were in fact more likely to be victims than causes
of social and urban decay. Many fell prey to unscrupulous landlords
who terrorised their tenants. One such was the notorious Perec
Rachman, who owned 147 properties in the Notting Hill area. In
1960 it was written that:

> Coloured people are feared as competitive intruders; they are
> thought of as promoters of crime and carriers of disease; they are
> resented when they are poor; they are envied when they are
> resourceful and thrifty. They are looked down upon; they are patro-
> nised; occasionally they are treated just like everyone else.[3]

Both inside and outside Parliament pressure grew for immigration
control. In the House of Commons Sir Cyril Osborne (Conservative,
Louth), Harold Gurden (Conservative, Birmingham Selly Oak) and
James Harrison (Labour, Nottingham West), among others, pressed
for immigration control. Osborne went so far as to state that 'it is time
someone spoke out for the white man in this country.'

In February 1961 he attempted to do just that by introducing a private member's bill to institute immigration control. The measure
suffered the fate of most private members' bills, and was defeated.

Osborne was, though, able to claim substantial backing for his bill, pointing to grass roots support among Conservative constituency associations. At the 1961 Conservative party conference, 39 anti-immigration motions were submitted. The conference overwhelmingly endorsed a motion calling for immigration control.

Outside Parliament, groups such as the Birmingham Immigration Control Association and the Southall Residents' Association were vociferous advocates of restriction. These groups seemed to tap a populist vein of support and even elicited approval from the Bishop of Birmingham who referred to West Indians as 'aliens' and 'a social burden'.

These campaigns, and their emotive imagery of 'invasions' and 'floods' had an effect on public opinion. The popular press also indulged in sensationalist reporting of the Nottingham and Notting Hill disturbances. In the aftermath of the Notting Hill anti-immigrant riots the *Daily Express* commissioned an opinion poll on attitudes to immigration control. Control was favoured by 79.1 per cent of respondents.

There is also evidence that the government was amenable to immigration control, and that it did not just slavishly follow public opinion. In 1955, the Conservative government actively considered immigration controls. It was, however, worried about the effects restriction would have on relations with New Commonwealth countries. However, pressure on the government grew as it failed to secure bilateral agreements with sending countries. In fact, in 1960 the Indian supreme court deemed it unlawful for the Indian government not to issue passports to those who wanted them.

At this time, the government was also having to consider ways of tackling Britain's relative political and economic decline. The retreat from Suez in 1956 dented world power pretensions, while the establishment of the European Economic Community by the Treaty of Rome in March 1957 prompted the government to consider whether Britain should throw its lot in with Europe, rather than seek to maintain its leading role in the Commonwealth.

THE COMMONWEALTH IMMIGRANTS BILL

In the early 1960s, pressure grew on the Conservative government to restrict New Commonwealth immigration. The 1961 queen's speech announced the government's intention to introduce a Commonwealth Immigrants Bill. The 1962 bill targeted certain kinds of immigrant. In particular it sought to restrict New Commonwealth – mainly black – immigration. Subsequent legislation in the 1960s, 1970s and 1980s further restricted New Commonwealth/black immigration.

This bill distinguished between citizens of the UK and its colonies, and citizens of independent Commonwealth countries. People who were not born in the UK, did not hold British passports issued by the UK government, or were not included on passports of people covered by the former categories were made subject to immigration controls. These controls took the form of vouchers issued by the Ministry of Labour. There were three types of voucher:

- **Category A** people who had a job to come to
- **Category B** people possessing specific skills in short supply, or very likely to get a job
- **Category C** other applicants, with priority given to ex-servicemen.

In 1963, 30 130 vouchers were issued. By 1972, the number issued had fallen to 2290.

At the bill's second reading on 16 November 1961 home secretary R A Butler justified immigration control on the grounds that as a result of the British Nationality Act 1948 'a sizeable part of the entire population of the earth' was entitled to come to Britain, which was already a densely populated country. Technically this was correct, but movement on such a scale was highly improbable. In fact, the demand for labour acted as a fairly good regulator of immigration during the 1950s. If there was a labour shortage immigration increased. If unemployment rose then labour migration tended to fall.

Butler was asked during the second reading debate about net migration, that is the number of people entering the country minus those leaving it. Such figures, showing both positive and negative net migration in the 1950s, tended to belie lurid imagery of 'invasions' and 'floods'. It was also reported that the UK economy had 300 000 job vacancies, although the government expressed concern about the economic slowdown and the implications of a large influx of unskilled and semi-skilled labour.

The bill passed into law as the Commonwealth Immigrants Act 1962, and provides a clear definition of the immigration 'problem'. It was

New Commonwealth immigration. The Act was the solution to the problem (as defined). The motive for the legislation was later revealed by government minister William Deedes when he wrote that, 'The Bill's real purpose was to restrict the influx of coloured immigrants. We were reluctant to say as much openly.'[4]

Labour opposed the legislation. Shadow home secretary Patrick Gordon Walker described the bill as 'bare faced, open race discrimination'. Labour claimed to be worried about the effects of the bill on Commonwealth relations, and also about the implications for domestic race relations of the introduction of a 'colour bar'. However, it was not long before Labour was also advocating control of New Commonwealth immigration.

THE BIPARTISAN CONSENSUS

Between 1962 and 1964 the policies of the two main parties on immigration and race issues converged. A coherent politics of race developed, characterised by bipartisan agreement on the need for control as a way of reducing the electoral significance of immigration.

Labour's change in policy was helped by the election of Harold Wilson as leader of the party following the untimely death of Hugh Gaitskell in January 1963. Gaitskell had vigorously opposed the Commonwealth Immigrants Bill. Wilson, though, announced that he was prepared to accept the need for statutory control. Labour's leadership was mindful of powerful anti-immigrant sentiment among voters in key constituencies in areas such as the West Midlands.

The point was drilled home by events in the Smethwick constituency at the October 1964 general election. Patrick Gordon Walker, shadow home secretary during the 1961 debates on immigration, was defending the seat for Labour. He was opposed by Conservative candidate Peter Griffiths who focused on Gordon Walker's 'softness' on immigration. Some of Griffiths' supporters used the slogan 'If you want a nigger neighbour, vote Labour'. Against a national swing of 3.2 per cent to Labour, Griffiths won the seat with a 7.5 per cent pro-Conservative swing. At the same general election anti-immigration candidates also did well in Southall and Birmingham Perry Bar, while anti-racism campaigner Fenner Brockway lost his Eton and Slough seat.

Cabinet minister Richard Crossman noted the potency of the anti-immigration/immigrant issue:

> Ever since the Smethwick election it has been quite clear that immigration can be the greatest political vote loser for the Labour Party if one seems to be permitting a flood of immigrants to come in and blight the central areas of our cities.[5]

Labour was determined not to be outflanked and sought to maintain a bipartisan policy with the Conservative frontbench, emphasising control of numbers of New Commonwealth immigrants. This was made clear by the 1965 white paper, *Immigration from the Commonwealth*, which reduced the number of employment vouchers to 8500. The white paper also created the National Committee for Commonwealth Immigrants (NCCI), which aimed to promote integration through the work of local voluntary organisations.

THE 'LIBERAL HOUR'

Labour's 1964 election manifesto also contained a pledge to enact legislation to tackle racial discrimination. It was this attempt to combine anti-discrimination legislation with measures to control numbers of New Commonwealth immigrants which was the hallmark of the 1960s race relations paradigm.

The period between 1964 and 1966 has been referred to as the 'liberal hour', because, for the first time, a government addressed itself to racism and took steps to tackle it. The intent of policy was captured by Roy Hattersley's famous aphorism, 'Without integration limitation is inexcusable: without limitation integration is impossible.' The aim of policy, according to home secretary Roy Jenkins, was not a 'flattening process of assimilation' but 'equal opportunity accompanied by cultural diversity'. It was this combination of control and a multicultural notion of integration that underpinned the bipartisan consensus between the Labour and Conservative leaderships.

An important drive behind the bipartisan consensus was Labour's fear that a populist Conservative party with an anti-immigration/immigrant stance would be electorally formidable. Consequently, Labour sought to 'depoliticise' race issues and remove them from the domain of party competition. It was decided that management of race and immigration issues should be devolved to the local level and made the work of voluntary organisations.

In 1965 the Labour government therefore secured enactment of the Race Relations Act, which made discrimination unlawful on the grounds of 'colour, race or ethnic or national origins'. The Act also made incitement to racial hatred a criminal offence. Its scope was, however, limited for two main reasons. First, it applied only to public places such as cinemas, public houses and restaurants. It did not apply to education, employment and housing, where discrimination was rife. Second, it did not invoke criminal sanctions against offenders. Rather, it relied on conciliation through the newly created Race Relations Board (RRB). The RRB was empowered to refer cases to the attorney general if conciliation did not work. However, the attorney general was never called upon.

The race relations framework created in the mid-1960s has been criticised on a number of grounds. From a radical perspective it has been argued that the principal intent of policy was control of New Commonwealth immigration and that attempts at integration were flawed if immigration policy was racist. How could a government tackle racism if it practised it through its own immigration policy? It has also been argued that race relations policy reifies ideas of race and gives them a meaning in debates about public policy which are not appropriate. Racism is the problem which should be tackled, rather than inflating to unjustified importance through race relations policy empty ideas of racial difference. From a conservative perspective race relations policy has been criticised because it attempted to use legislation as an instrument of social engineering. Critics of the legislation, such as Enoch Powell, played on fears of a 'race police' monitoring people's attitudes. It was also felt that immigrants had an obligation to assimilate to some notion of the 'British way of life' and, by implication, leave if they were not prepared to do so.

INTEGRATION OR CONTROL?

During the 'liberal hour' the 1965 Act was criticised for not going far enough in terms of anti-racism legislation. Indeed, home secretary Roy Jenkins encouraged debate about extension of the scope of race relations legislation. However, his attempt to foster debate of anti-racism legislation was overshadowed by the public response to a sudden influx in 1967-68 of 13 000 East African Asians who left Kenya because of its 'Africanisation' policy.

Thus, the issue of New Commonwealth immigration returned to the centre of political debate in 1967 and 1968. In particular, Jenkins' view of a plural, multicultural Britain was challenged by Enoch Powell's emphasis on the maintenance of cultural homogeneity based on preservation of 'British national identity', and his apocalyptic warning of the effects of continued immigration. Powell foresaw 'race war', and pointed to disturbances in American cities as evidence of what could happen in Britain.

As a result, Labour moved quickly to restrict immigration by East African Asians. The Commonwealth Immigrants Act 1968, rushed through Parliament in only three days, extended immigration control to East African Asians. It did so through a patriality rule which decreed that, to enter the UK, Commonwealth immigrants needed close ties, meaning at least one parent or grandparent born, adopted, naturalised or registered as a UK citizen. The Act, it has been argued, was 'the logical outcome of Labour's policy of appeasement'.[6]

The government was bitterly criticised for its actions. A *Times* leader described the Act as 'probably the most shameful measure that the Labour members have ever been asked by their whip to support.' Labour MP Andrew Faulds remarked, 'That a Socialist Government should be responsible fills me with shame and despair.'

The 1968 Act demonstrated two things. First, it made very clear Labour's concern to be seen to be 'tough' on immigration. Indeed, Labour's 'toughness' led to legislation that was perhaps more severe than a Conservative government would have introduced. Second, it confirmed that race relations policy was predicated upon control of numbers. The assumption of policy was that control of numbers would lead to better race relations. The logic of this argument was that race relations would improve if immigration was tightly controlled. However, only a certain type of immigration – from the New Commonwealth – was really made subject to these controls.

Nevertheless, in 1968 the government further extended the scope of anti-discrimination legislation. In 1967 a report by Political and Economic Planning had revealed systematic racial discrimination. Although the impetus Jenkins had hoped to build in favour of anti-discrimination legislation was overshadowed by the Kenyan Asians issue, a Race Relations Bill was presented to the House of Commons a few weeks after passage of the Commonwealth Immigrants Act 1968. It extended the scope of the 1965 Act to cover employment, housing, education and the provision of goods, facilities and services to the public. The Act also created the Community Relations Commission (CRC), which replaced the NCCI and coordinated the work of local voluntary community relations organisations.

DEVELOPMENTS IN THE 1970s

In the 1970s the race relations policy paradigm was consolidated. The Conservatives' Immigration Act 1971 effectively ended primary immigration and Labour's Race Relations Act 1976 extended the scope of the 1968 race relations legislation.

On the control side of debate, constituency Conservative associations continued to press for tighter immigration controls. In 1968 the Conservative Political Centre found that 327 out of 412 surveyed constituency associations wanted all immigration to stop indefinitely, while a further 55 favoured a five-year ban on new immigration. Politicisation and racialisation of the immigration issue by Enoch Powell in the same year reaped an electoral dividend for the Conservatives in the 1970 general election. Even though Powell was immediately sacked from the Conservative frontbench after making his April 1968 'rivers of blood speech', he helped to establish a perception in voters' minds that the Conservatives were 'tough' on immigration. The Conservatives' 1970 general election manifesto contained a pledge to tighten immigration controls and to provide assistance for voluntary repatriation.

Indeed, immigration was the fourth most important issue for voters in the 1970 election, and contributed to the Conservative victory. The Immigration Act 1971 made good the Tory pledge further to restrict immigration. It replaced all preceding legislation with one statute. The Act distinguished between citizens of the UK and colonies who were patrial (according to the criteria introduced by the 1968 legislation) and had the right to settle in Britain, and non-patrials who did not. For non-patrials, the legislation replaced vouchers with work permits which did not give right of permanent residence and were renewable annually.

On the integration side of debate, the Labour government passed the Race Relations Act 1976. This extended the scope of the 1968 legislation to cover indirect as well as direct racial discrimination. Direct discrimination – whereby a person treats another less favourably on racial grounds – was already covered by the 1968 legislation. However, it was clear that indirect discrimination – whereby treatment is equal in a formal sense between groups but discriminatory in its effects on one group – was also a serious problem. Housing allocation criteria could, for example, stipulate residence qualifications which were supposedly the same for everyone but which could in fact discriminate against recent immigrants. The Act also defined discrimination to allow scope for positive action to overcome the effects of past discrimination. This permitted the government to develop training programmes to equip ethnic minorities for areas of work from which they had traditionally been excluded. Positive discrimination, whereby on the basis of ethnic origin people are appointed to jobs or allowed access to education, housing and so on, remained illegal. The 1976 Act also created the Commission for Racial Equality (CRE) to undertake tasks previously performed by the RRB and the CRC.

The mid-1970s actually witnessed three pieces of equality legislation. The Sex Discrimination Act 1975 was the pathbreaker for the Race Relations Act 1976. The Fair Employment (Northern Ireland) Act 1976 outlawed discrimination on grounds of religious belief or political opinion in the province. It has been argued that these Acts led to a 'fragmentation of the principle of equality which... is absurd. Only a black, Catholic woman can enjoy the protection of all three measures irrespective of the part of the country in which she may happen to be.'[7]

THE 'PROBLEM' OF IMMIGRATION

Race relations policy is an example of governmental problem-solving. Perception of the problem did not extend to all types of immigration. Rather it was immigration from the New Commonwealth and Pakistan that was viewed as problematic. In the 1960s and 1970s, British race relations policy was predicated on the perceived need to restrict immigration from these countries. Hostility towards immigrants from these countries was fuelled to a large extent by racism. Legislation to tackle racism followed in the wake of steps to tighten controls in line with the assumption that good race relations could not be established without control of numbers.

The 1960s and 1970s thus saw the establishment of Britain's race relations policy. The hallmark of policy development was bipartisan
agreement on tight immigration controls and measures to promote
integration of settled immigrants and their descendants. Both the
Labour and the Conservative leaderships subscribed to this policy
framework. Labour was particularly fearful of damaging electoral consequences if it was seen to be 'soft' on immigration.

British race relations policy thus sought to neutralise issues of immigration and race, and to reduce their electoral salience. However,
attempts to exclude the immigration issue from politics also had the
effect of excluding immigrants and their descendants from participation in policy debates. This undesirable consequence of the depoliticisation implicit in race relations policy has only comparatively recently
been addressed through increased ethnic minority political participation. People from ethnic minorities became public policy 'objects'
rather than 'actors' and found themselves largely excluded from key
debates about matters of direct relevance to themselves.[8] These issues
are examined in the next two chapters.

NOTES

1. B Carter, C Harris and S Joshi, 'The 1951-55 Conservative Government and the
Racialisation of Black Immigration', *Policy Papers in Ethnic Relations* 11 (Centre for
Research in Ethnic Relations, University of Warwick, 1987).
2. Fryer, op cit, p381.
3. R Glass and H Pollins, *Newcomers: The West Indians in London* (Allen and Unwin,
London, 1960), p120.
4. W F Deedes, *Race Without Rancour* (Conservative Political Centre, London, 1968),
p10.
5. R Crossman, *The Diaries of a Cabinet Minister*, vol 1 (Hamish Hamilton and Jonathan
Cape, London, 1975), pp149-50.
6. Layton-Henry, op cit, p79.
7. A Lester, 'Anti-discrimination Legislation in Great Britain', *New Community* 14 (1987),
p24.
8. J Crowley, 'Paradoxes in the Politicisation of Race: A Comparison of the UK and
France', *New Community* 19 (1993), pp627-44.

5 PLAYING THE RACE CARD? THE CONSERVATIVES AND IMMIGRATION

Conservative party thinking and policy are central to consideration of the politics of immigration and race, for the simple reason that the Conservatives are the most successful political party in modern Britain. They have formed governments for 34 of the 51 years since the second world war, and in the 1960s and 1970s were central to formulation of the race relations paradigm. The party's stance on immigration and race is surveyed in this chapter.

CONSERVATISM AND RACE RELATIONS

The Conservative party, like most other major parties, is a broad church. Within the party are different strands of thinking which, although according with Conservatism's central tenets, emphasise different elements within it. On issues of immigration and race, different wings of the party stress distinct responses to particular issues. During the 1960s the Conservative and Labour leaderships agreed on the main features of race relations policy. However, there is evidence that this elite-level agreement did not reach down to the grass roots.

Indeed, in the 1960s substantial antipathy towards immigration and immigrants was apparent within the Conservative party. In 1968 Enoch Powell touched a populist nerve with his anti-immigration rhetoric. Following her election as leader of the party in 1975, Margaret Thatcher also displayed populist instincts as she articulated what she believed to be the concerns of grass roots Conservatives. After Thatcher became party leader in 1975, immigration and race issues were repoliticised.

In surveying Conservatism and race, the views of Powell and Thatcher are particularly important. In more recent years, 'Europeanisation' of the immigration issue has required a response from the Major government. It has occurred because of the EU's attempts to promote free movement of people within the Union, and has generated a largely negative response from Conservatives.

POWELLISM

Enoch Powell, Conservative MP for Wolverhampton South West between 1950 and 1974, was for many years at the forefront of Tory opposition to immigration. Indeed, his anti-immigration/immigrant campaign attracted support from both Conservative and Labour voters. Even though the party leadership officially disowned his views and sacked him from his frontbench position, he influenced the party's views on the subject for many years.

Powell's opposition to black immigration capitalised on concerns that had long been evident within the Conservative party. In the 1950s the Conservative government had considered the need for control of black immigration, despite labour shortages. In fact, as health minister between 1960 and 1963, Powell welcomed West Indian immigrants to work in the National Health Service and counter labour shortages. In later years, the economic importance of immigration was something that Powell and others preferred not to stress. In the 1960s extra-parliamentary anti-immigration campaigns such as the Birmingham Immigration Control Association and the Southall Residents' Association, had prominent Conservatives among their members. At the 1964 general election the strength of hostility towards immigrants was clearly evident at Smethwick.

It was in the late 1960s that Powell became increasingly unhappy about the effects of black immigration. He was constrained in his actions by membership of Edward Heath's shadow cabinet, but this did not stop him from voicing his opposition to Kenyan Asian immigration in 1967-68. Indeed, he vigorously opposed this immigration on the grounds that continued admission of culturally distinct people would destroy the cultural homogeneity which he believed to be a fundamental strength of the British nation. He also foresaw violent confrontation – 'race war' – if large-scale immigration continued. In support of his views, he pointed to riots in American cities.

Powell's anti-immigration politics stemmed from his perception of 'Britishness', although it might be said that they were in many ways more reflective of aspects of 'Englishness'. Almost by definition, black people could not share in the culture, values and tradition of what was implicitly a white 'British' identity. Thus, although Powell might claim that he was not a racist, the implication of his views was that British national identity was linked to cultural and racial homogeneity.

For Powell continued immigration was 'like a nation busily engaged in heaping up its own funeral pyre'. Powellites argued that the 'British nation' (or to be more precise their particular conception of the 'British nation' and 'Britishness') could only be preserved by ending immigration and instituting repatriation for already-settled immigrants. Powellism presented a fundamental challenge to the liberal notion of multiculturalism which was an aspect of race relations policy. In a manner reminiscent of backing for the British Brothers' League earlier in the century, London dockers and meat porters marched in support of Powell following his 'rivers of blood' speech, given in Wolverhampton in April 1968.

Powell's speech led to his immediate sacking from the Conservative frontbench, and party leader Edward Heath dissociated himself from Powell's views. However, the effect of Powell's repoliticisation of the immigration issue was to increase Conservative support, as it was seen as the party that was 'tough' on immigration.[1] Powell demonstrated the electoral potential for a Tory leader prepared to play the 'race card'. In the 1970s, Margaret Thatcher learned the lesson.

Heath, though, was determined to maintain the bipartisan approach, arguing that 'there is no reason why cultural diversity should not be combined with loyalty to this country'. Nevertheless, the 1970 Conservative general election manifesto did make it clear that the party intended to institute tight control of immigration. The resultant Immigration Act 1971 effectively ended primary immigration. Despite this, Heath earnt some plaudits, and the bitter condemnation of Powell, when in 1972 he sanctioned entry of Ugandan Asians expelled by General Amin. His action was in contrast to Labour's response to the Kenyan Asian crisis of 1967-68, and indicates that the Conservatives were not uniquely illiberal in their immigration policy.

THATCHER AND THE 'NEW RIGHT'

Once the Conservatives had been defeated for the second time in a matter of months at the October 1974 general election, Heath was challenged for the leadership of the party by former education secretary, Margaret Thatcher. In February 1975 Thatcher became Conservative party leader. She was, as she frequently made clear, a conviction politician. In particular, she rejected the consensus politics which she saw as a major contributor to Britain's post-war economic and political decline. One aspect of the post-war consensus was race relations policy, with both main parties agreeing on the principal features of policy as a way of reducing the electoral salience of the immigration issue. Following her election as leader, Thatcher repoliticised immigration. She sought tighter controls on secondary immigrants. She also articulated ideas about British national identity which had a distinctly Powellite tone.

Thatcher's populism was based on what she saw as the concerns of ordinary people. In the 1970s, despite the implementation of restrictive legislation, there was still evidence of continued public concern about immigration. Thatcher was prepared to capitalise on these anxieties and appeal to anti-immigration/immigrant sentiment to win votes. Her views on immigration and race relations were made clear in the years leading up to the 1979 general election.

In 1976 Thatcher opposed the Race Relations Bill, though her position was undermined by a Conservative backbench revolt. In 1977 she sought to veto Conservative participation in the all-party Joint Campaign Against Racialism (JCAR), seeing it as a left-wing front organisation. This was despite the fact that many participants were bastions of respectability, including the British Council of Churches, the Board of Deputies of British Jews and the British Youth Services. Thatcher's opposition prompted a rift between herself and the executive committee of the Conservative party's National Union, which in fact went ahead and appointed Sheelagh Roberts to the JCAR. In January 1978 Thatcher nailed her populist colours firmly to the mast in an interview on the Granada Television programme *World in Action*. During the interview she made it clear that her role was to act upon people's concerns rather than ignore them: 'if you want good race relations you have got to allay people's fears on numbers.' She also said that she thought that people were 'really rather afraid that the country might be swamped by people with a different culture', and contended that the failure of governments to take a tough line on immigration was driving people to support the extreme right-wing National Front.

Thatcher was criticised for these remarks by liberal journalists. In the *Times* Bernard Levin wrote that:

> If you talk and behave as though black men were some kind of virus that must be kept out of reach of the body politic then it is the shabbiest hypocrisy to preach racial harmony at the same time.[2]

However, Thatcher received about 10 000 letters of support from Conservative and Labour voters. The Conservatives also moved from level-pegging with Labour into a commanding 9 per cent opinion poll lead immediately after the interview. At the time, 21 per cent of those questioned said that they thought immigration was one of the two most pressing issues facing the country. In February 1978 the Conservatives won the Ilford North by-election from Labour. There seemed plenty of electoral mileage in the 'race card', and Thatcher's populist right-wing instincts allowed her to maximise Tory advantage as the 'tough' party on immigration.

THE NATIONAL FRONT

Conservative activity in the mid-1970s took place against a background of racist mobilisation. Throughout the 1970s the NF sought to profit from anti-immigration sentiment by arguing for an end to immigration and repatriation of already-settled black immigrants. Some of its electoral performances, such as its 4789 votes (16.3 per cent) in the 1973 West Bromwich by-election, prompted suggestions that it could replace the Liberals as the third largest party.

These fears turned out to be unfounded, as the NF never managed to have a single candidate elected to either a local council or Parliament. Nevertheless, when assessing its impact it is important to bear in mind the response of the main political parties. It could be argued that Thatcher's *World in Action* interview sought to appeal to Tory voters attracted by the NF's anti-immigration stance. In this way the NF may have influenced an important aspect of the policy of the Conservative government elected in 1979.

The NF was founded in 1967 from a disparate group of extreme-right organisations such as the League of Empire Loyalists and the British National Party. Its vigorous opposition to immigration saw it acquire a niche in the electoral marketplace. It polled strongly in local elections in the mid-1970s without winning any seats. In Blackburn, however, the breakaway National Party gained two council seats in 1976.

The extreme right's local election 'success' was aided by sensationalist reporting of the entry to the UK of several thousand Malawian Asians in 1976. Accommodation of some recent arrivals in a four-star hotel in Sussex enabled sections of the tabloid press to wax indignant.

At its peak, the NF attracted working-class voters from both the Conservatives and Labour. Its working-class support has been linked to inner-city social and economic restructuring which prompted alienation from traditional electoral allegiances.[3] In addition, in some parts of the UK, such as the East End of London, there is almost a tradition both of immigration and of support for the extreme right. Support for the NF was particularly evident in parts of the country with large immigrant settlement. It also performed well in areas neighbouring those with immigrant populations. A parallel 'halo effect' has been seen in support for Jean-Marie Le Pen's Front National in France.

Towards the end of the 1970s NF support waned. Its neo-fascist politics were challenged by organisations such as Rock Against Racism and the Anti-Nazi League, which were particularly effective in discrediting the extreme right in the eyes of young people. The NF was not only challenged in the realm of ideas. NF marches prompted anti-racist and anti-fascist counter-mobilisation. Many of these confrontations led to violence which also helped to discredit NF claims to be a party of 'law and order'. Former Conservative and Labour voters attracted by the NF's 'tough' stance on immigration were repelled by its violent and anti-democratic nature. The seeds of NF decline were thus sown prior to Thatcher's 'swamping' statement. These remarks merely stole its thunder and made it clear that the Conservatives were the 'tough' party on immigration.

The NF had little else to fall back on as it was solely defined by its stance on immigration. It was obliterated in the 1979 general election, when it fielded 303 candidates, thereby gaining access to television and radio airtime for its views. In total, however, NF candidates won only 0.6 per cent of the vote. The NF even performed badly in traditional East End strongholds. Following this electoral debacle the NF splintered and declined further. In the 1990s one successor party, the British National Party, has enjoyed some success, winning a local council seat in Tower Hamlets in 1993.

Some former NF members joined the Conservative party. In 1983 a Young Conservative report revealed the extent of infiltration and the links between the Tory right and the extreme right. In the 1983 general election there was embarrassment for the Conservatives when Stockton South candidate, Thomas Finnegan, was found to be a former NF candidate. He was shunned by party leaders who refused to campaign on his behalf, and he lost a seat he was expected to win.

There was also relief amongst party leaders when the annual confer-ence overwhelmingly rejected a motion from the Billericay Conserva-tive Association calling for repatriation of immigrants and repeal of all race relations legislation.

THE FIRST THATCHER GOVERNMENT, 1979-83

The Conservatives' 1979 general election manifesto contained what shadow home secretary William Whitelaw called further 'tough but fair' immigration policies. In particular, it proposed measures to curtail secondary immigration. In government the party also sought to re-define British citizenship by means of the British Nationality Act 1981.

In office, however, the first Thatcher government found its election-eering anti-immigration rhetoric tempered by the reality of construct-ing a coherent and feasible policy. The Conservatives' 1979 manifesto contained a number of proposals intended to reduce secondary immi-gration. These included introduction of an immigration quota; restric-tions on entry of children, parents and grandparents to those with compassionate reasons for entering Britain; withdrawal of the conces-sion made by the Labour government in 1974 allowing entry of hus-bands and male fiancés; and establishment of a register of depen-dents eligible to settle in Britain. Nevertheless, there were problems in drafting legislation. A register of dependents was likely both to be very difficult to establish and to offend Commonwealth governments, particularly the Indian. The impracticalities of an immigration quota were also pointed out, as was the fact that restrictions on entry for marriage were likely to hit white people just as hard as blacks, which was not what the legislation was intended to do.

The new immigration rules laid before the House of Commons in November 1979 attempted to clamp down on 'marriages of conve-nience', while elderly dependents were only to be admitted if they were dependent on relatives already in Britain and had a standard of living below the average in their own country. This latter condition was unlikely to be met as most such dependents received money from relatives in the UK.

Labour opposed the new immigration rules, arguing that they were racially discriminatory and contravened the principle that all British citizens should be treated equally. There was also opposition from some Conservative backbenchers to restrictions on immigration by elderly dependents. In response to its critics, the government presented its final statement on immigration rules to the Commons in February 1980. The proposed rules on entry for marriage and settlement by elderly dependents had been relaxed.

The government then turned its attention to citizenship legislation. The British Nationality Act 1981 steered British citizenship policy further away from the 'imperial' model established by the British Nationality Act 1948, which gave citizens of former colonies the right to settle in Britain. By withdrawing this right, the government brought British nationality law into line with that in other European countries, reflecting the change in Britain's international status.

The 1981 Act moved towards the principle of *jus sanguinis* – qualification for citizenship by virtue of descent from British citizens – and away from *jus soli* – qualification by birth in Britain. Home secretary William Whitelaw argued that just because a person was born in Britain did not mean that he or she should be entitled to British citizenship. However, the shift made by the government was not in the end as radical as it had initially intended. Following protests made after the bill's first reading in the Commons, amendments to the legislation allowed those born in the UK whose parents were not citizens to acquire citizenship after 10 years' residence, and for naturalised British citizens to transmit citizenship to their descendants.

The British Nationality Act 1981 created three types of British citizen:
- British citizenship for those with close ties to Britain. 'Close ties' meant that person who was born, adopted, naturalised or registered in Britain; born to or legally adopted by a parent or grandparent coming into the preceding category; or had been, before 1 January 1983, ordinarily resident continuously in Britain for five years and had been settled at the end of that period.
- British dependent territories citizenship for people connected with dependent territories such as the Falkland Islands, Gibraltar and Hong Kong who had acquired that status as a result of their own, their parents' or their grandparents' birth in a dependency or associated state.
- British overseas citizenship, a residual category to which almost no rights were attached. It applied particularly to East African Asians and Malaysians and was designed to encourage them to acquire citizenship in their country of permanent residence.

This Act became law on 1 January 1983. A controversial House of Lords amendment allowed special access to British citizenship for Gibraltarians. Equivalent access was extended to Falkland Islanders after the war with Argentina.

Taken together with tightening of the immigration rules, the actions of the first Thatcher government have been seen as putting an end to the immigration issue in British politics. As will be shown later, Europeanisation of the issue means that this may not in fact be the case. However, at the 1983 general election immigration attracted little attention. The government was able to point to the severe restrictions it had put in place, and to argue that acceptances for settlement, which had fallen between 1973 and 1983, had shown a particularly noticeable decline after 1979 (Table 5.1).

Table 5.1 Acceptances for settlement in Britain, 1973-83

	1973 '000	1976 '000	1979 '000	1980 '000	1981 '000	1982 '000	1983 '000
NCWP	30.3	55.1	37.2	33.7	31.4	30.4	27.5
Total	55.2	80.7	70.7	69.7	58.1	53.8	53.5

Source Control of Immigration statistics

URBAN UNREST

The years of the first Thatcher government saw substantial increases in unemployment. The alienation and marginalisation prompted by economic inactivity were linked to unrest in many of Britain's cities in the early 1980s. These disturbances were labelled 'race riots', even though people with different ethnic origins took part in the disturbances and despite the fact that socio-economic conditions, compounded by racism, were of far greater importance in triggering unrest than were supposed racial differences.

The first outbreak of disorder occurred in the St Pauls area of Bristol in 1980. This was followed by serious disturbances in Brixton (London) and Toxteth (Liverpool) in 1981. There were also disturbances in other British towns and cities. Following the 1981 unrest Lord Scarman was commissioned by the government to investigate the causes of the Brixton disturbances. His report called into question many precepts of government policy. Scarman's report blamed both the police and community leaders for the disturbances. He rejected the idea of institutional racism, but did point to incidences of misconduct which could be construed as racist. Scarman made links between deprivation and repressive policing which 'created a predisposition towards violent protest'. He proposed reform of aspects of policing, such as the complaints procedure. He also sought action to tackle the fundamental social inequalities that he believed to underpin the tension in inner-city areas.[4] However, such responses ran against the grain of the Thatcherite laissez-faire approach. Despite the fact that environment secretary Michael Heseltine assumed special responsibility for economic regeneration on Merseyside, little was done about Scarman's report.

The unrest did however prompt renewed debate about the long-term effects of immigration. In the House of Commons, Roy Hattersley's view that unrest could be linked to social deprivation and unemployment was challenged by Enoch Powell. He linked the disorder to his earlier grim prophesies of 'race war' and contended that:

> There is a factor, the factor which the people concerned perfectly well know, understand and apprehend, and that unless it can be dealt with – unless the fateful inevitability, the inexorable doubling and trebling of that element of a population can be avoided – their worst fears will be fulfilled.[5]

Renewed unrest in the Lozells area of Birmingham and on the Broadwater Farm estate in Haringey, London, in 1985 provoked further debate. It was extended by the death of two Asian shopkeepers in Lozells and the murder of a policeman in Haringey. The Conservative government preferred to emphasise individual lawlessness rather than give credence to explanations focusing on poverty, deprivation and unemployment.

A JANUS-FACED APPROACH?

While adopting illiberal immigration controls which discriminated against Asian and Afro-Caribbean people the Conservatives also sought to woo sections of the growing ethnic minority electorate. In particular, they sought to cultivate support among sections of the Asian population.

In 1976 a Community Affairs Department was established at Conservative Central Office. Within it was an ethnic minorities unit which created two associations for Conservatives from ethnic minorities. The Anglo-Asian Conservative Society was the more successful of the two. At its peak in the early 1980s it had about 30 branches. The Anglo-West Indian Conservative Society was less successful. It was concentrated in London and never had more than 10 branches. The societies aimed to integrate Conservatives from ethnic minorities into the party. The idea of separate sections, along the lines of Labour's black sections, was inimical to Tories. However, the organisations were represented on local and national committees of the National Union of Conservative and Unionist Associations.

By 1986 the two societies had been dissolved, mainly because of strife within the Anglo-Asian society over the creation of an independent Sikh homeland. They were replaced by the One Nation Forum. Membership of the Forum was by invitation only: 'Most of its political activities coincide with social functions serving chiefly as useful networking opportunities for ambitious black Tories.'[6] Despite these small-scale attempts on the part of the Conservative party to appear more sympathetic to the needs of its ethnic minority supporters, the Labour Party retained the support of the overwhelming majority of ethnic minority voters. The Conservatives were far more interested, and successful, in appealing to white working class voters worried about the 'threat' of immigration than they were in courting the votes of the ethnic minority electorate.

EUROPEANISATION OF THE IMMIGRATION ISSUE

At the time, it was thought that the 1983 general election marked the end of the immigration issue. However, in the 1990s immigration has acquired heightened salience as a result of Britain's EU membership. John Major's government has had to cope with opposition to two 'threats' to British sovereignty: European integration and immigration. Some politicians who were opposed to immigration, such as Enoch Powell's successor in Wolverhampton South West, Nicholas Budgen, have also become prominent 'Eurosceptics'.

Europeanisation of the immigration issue was driven chiefly by the 1986 Single European Act (SEA), which sought to establish a single European market within which people, services, goods and capital could move freely. The Conservative government has always been sceptical about provisions for free movement of people. One reason for this is its fear of losing its ability to maintain strict entry controls. If a common EU immigration policy were to develop then Britain's external frontier would be in countries like Italy. The British government remains unconvinced about the ability of Italians effectively to police their external frontier.

The SEA in fact contained a clause which made development of a single European immigration policy unlikely. Britain also refused to participate in the Schengen group of EU member states which have decided to create a free movement area. On 26 March 1995 Belgium, France, Germany, Luxembourg, the Netherlands, Portugal and Spain ended passport controls for their nationals. France subsequently suspended its membership in July 1995 because of concern about increased drug trafficking resulting from liberal Dutch laws. The French extreme right was also vocal in calling for tighter controls. Le Pen's Front National is vociferously anti-immigration/immigrant, while Philippe de Villiers, another right-wing presidential candidate in 1995, campaigned against the removal of border controls.

In spite of its opposition to free movement of people, Britain did sign (in 1991) and ratify (in 1993) the Maastricht Treaty which contains provisions for development of an EU interior policy, including immigration and asylum policy. Chapter 8 looks at ways in which common decision-making at EU level affects Britain's traditional thinking about immigration policy. Historically, the ability of states to control movement of people into and out of their territory has been an important aspect of national sovereignty. This is no longer the case for EU member states which are Schengen signatories. Immigration has become entangled with the politically explosive European issue, and is likely to present British governments with complex problems in years to come.

A LURCH TO THE RIGHT?

In 1995, claims were made that the Conservative government was becoming increasingly right-wing. An important aspect of this view was that policies on asylum and immigration pandered to racism and xenophobia. In its November 1995 queen's speech, the Conservative government outlined policies which would make it even more difficult for asylum-seekers who wished to remain in Britain. Among these proposals was a plan to withdraw Social Security benefits from 13 000 asylum seekers from 8 January 1996, although the plan was postponed to allow time for parliamentary review. The CRE condemned the plans as 'anti-black and xenophobic' while the Refugee Council contended that the proposed new regulations would put 8000 people out on the street with no money for food. Another feature of the proposals was the drawing-up of a 'white list' of countries deemed 'safe'. The fact that Nigeria had appeared on an early version of this list caused some embarrassment following the execution in November 1995 of human rights activist Ken Saro-Wiwa by the military regime.

This confirmation of the restrictive nature of Conservative immigration and asylum policy ties in with other aspects of policy, such as welfare, that are seen as motivated by right-wing ideas. Conservative leaders have also been keen to portray themselves as defenders of the 'natural interest', or at least their particular conception of it. Defence secretary Michael Portillo's speech to the 1995 party conference was widely condemned as xenophobic. The Conservative government was also reluctant to join with other EU member states in a declaration against racism and xenophobia which, among other things, sought to make denial of the holocaust an indictable offence. The British government claimed that the measures were unlikely to improve on the perceived success of British race relations policy.

Even though prime minister John Major claims that the Conservatives still occupy the centre-right of British politics, it could be argued that the Tories have reaped a Thatcherite whirlwind. Contained within its destructive swirl is a strident, aggressive, nationalistic and potentially xenophobic brand of policy that became influential in the mid-1990s.

THE IMPACT OF CONSERVATISM

Under Margaret Thatcher's leadership the Conservatives renounced post-war consensus politics. One feature of the consensus was race relations policy. Thatcher eschewed bipartisanship, preferring to advance Powellite ideas about British nationality and immigration which had the effect of repoliticising these issues. The Conservatives were able to portray themselves as 'tough' on immigration and to gain some electoral advantage over the Labour Party by playing the 'race card'.

Between 1979 and 1983 legislation severely restricted secondary immigration into the UK and redefined British citizenship. Despite

Thatcher's nationalistic rhetoric, this redefinition was a tacit recognition of Britain's reduced status in the world, and its decline from an imperial to a middle-ranking European power. However, these policy changes introduced by the first Thatcher administration may not have 'ended' the immigration issue because European integration and provision for free movement of people are raising the salience of the immigration issue during the Major premiership.

The participatory effects of Conservative policy are also interesting. By seeking to portray themselves as 'tough' on immigration in the late 1970s and 1980s, the Conservatives distanced themselves from the concerns of many people from ethnic minorities. In particular, by embracing aspects of the Powellite agenda, the Conservatives subscribed to views on national identity which excluded many immigrants and their descendants. Under Thatcher the Conservatives preferred to attract support from white anti-immigration voters rather than appeal to the small ethnic minority electorate, many members of which were in any case unlikely to be Conservative supporters.

NOTES

1. D Studlar, 'British Public Opinion, Colour Issues and Enoch Powell: A Longitudinal Analysis', *British Journal of Political Science* 4 (1974), pp371-81.
2. Quoted in Layton-Henry, op cit, p186.
3. A Phizacklea and R Miles, *Labour and Racism* (Routledge, London, 1980).
4. Lord Scarman, *The Brixton Disorders, 10-12 April 1981: Report of an Inquiry*, Cmnd 8427 (HMSO, London, 1981).
5. Quoted in Solomos, op cit, p105.
6. T Sewell, *Black Tribunes: Black Political Participation in Britain* (Lawrence and Wishart, London, 1993), p66.

6 RACE RELATIONS, ANTI-RACISM AND THE LABOUR PARTY

In the 1960s a bipartisan race relations policy was seen as being in Labour's best interests because it 'neutralised' the immigration issue by partially extracting it from the domain of two-party competition. Labour's opposition to immigration control in 1961 and 1962 was superseded by concern about the electoral effects of being seen to be 'soft' on immigration, dramatically revealed by the loss of Smethwick in the 1964 general election. A consequence of this was that Labour became willing to adopt hard-line measures as a means of maintaining anti-immigration credibility. Although Labour enacted race relations legislation in 1965 and 1968, it also passed a restrictive measure in 1968. Labour's subsequent stance on race is investigated here.

THE ORIGINS OF LABOUR POLICY

Race relations policy, as well as debates both between and within the main political parties, had adverse participatory effects on ethnic minorities. Despite holding the same formal political rights as other British citizens, people from these minorities were largely excluded from the formal political process. In the 1970s there were very few local councillors and no MPs from ethnic minority groups.

In the 1970s and 1980s political activists sought to remedy this deficiency. In particular, more people from minority ethnic groups became active in the Labour Party, which attracted the bulk of the ethnic minority vote. Attempts were made to increase Labour's representativeness through selection and election of more local councillors and MPs from ethnic minorities. Labour was also influenced by anti-racist ideas, particularly at local government level. These debates about greater participation, more effective representation and development of new policy agendas culminated in the contentious issue of the establishment of black sections within the party based on the principle of self-organisation.

The origins and effects of the black sections debate are key to understanding the sources and development of Labour policy. Labour underwent dramatic changes in the 1970s and 1980s, moving to the left after the 1979 general election defeat under the leadership of Michael Foot and the ideological influence of former cabinet minister Tony Benn. Following the crushing 1983 general election defeat the new party leader, Neil Kinnock, sought to 'modernise' the party and make it more electable. One effect of this was to marginalise the black sections movement associated with the 'hard left'. Later parts of this chapter will investigate this aspect of Labour politics in detail.

LABOUR AND RACE RELATIONS

Labour played a central role in developing race relations policy. Under Hugh Gaitskell in the early 1960s the party opposed the Common- wealth Immigrants Act 1962 because it thought that the legislation would damage the Commonwealth and harm domestic race rela- tions. Following Gaitskell's death and Harold Wilson's election as party leader early in 1963 it became clear that Labour was prepared to sup- port immigration control, coupled with legislation to combat discrimi- nation. Labour reduced the number of employment vouchers made available and responded illiberally to immigration by Kenyan Asians in 1968. The Race Relations Acts 1965 and 1968 outlawed certain mani- festations of discrimination and devolved responsibility for manage- ment of race relations to local organisations, such as Community Relations Councils.

'Good' race relations was predicated upon tight control of numbers and was not a 'chicken and egg' policy. It is quite clear that immi- gration control came first. In accepting this problematisation of the immigration issue Labour was yielding to political pressures. In Smethwick the power of anti-immigration sentiment, as well as the dangers of appearing to be too 'soft' on immigration, were made clear. The strength of anti-immigration feeling, and its strong roots among the working classes, was evident in support for Enoch Powell. London dockers and meat porters marched in support of Powell and he received clear support for his views from anti-immigration Labour voters.

Within the Labour Party there was support for immigration control from trade unions, such as the Transport and General Workers' Union, who feared that immigrants would act as a cheap pool of labour and undercut their members' pay. Even though official union policy and many officials strongly opposed discrimination in the workplace, they found some members colluding with management in discrimination against workers of immigrant origin.

In the 1950s and early 1960s Fenner Brockway, Labour MP for Windsor and Eton until 1964, pressed for anti-discrimination legislation. Whether such anti-discriminatory zeal extended to the party's grass roots is debatable. The following is an extract from the minutes of a meeting of the Bedford Divisional Labour Party in 1967. It is clearly not a definitive statement of Labour members' views but does give some indication of the nature of discussions on immigration in the 1960s.

> A member said that we might just as well give the whole damn country to the blacks as they would get it in the end anyway. Before long we would have a black King on the throne and then it would be God help us! The poor old white man might just as well emigrate and leave the place to them.
>
> He said that this black menace had ruined our towns and forced the whites out of them. The best thing we could do would be to send the whole damn lot of them back to where they came from!
>
> Mr Storrow said that he was not aware that Ian Smith [prime minister of Rhodesia] was present but apparently he was...
>
> Mr Whittle said that they must learn to reject some of their ways. Some of them would gladly do without education for their children and street lighting, etc if it saved them paying rates and taxes. We were gradually winning the battle but it was a long fight...

Labour felt itself to be vulnerable on issues of race and immigration. It sought to reduce their salience by securing bipartisan agreement on race relations policy. Powell's outspoken attack on the policy framework showed Labour's continued vulnerability. Even though Powell was disowned by his party leadership his views strengthened voters' perceptions of the Conservatives as the 'tough' party on immigration and contributed to their 1970 general election victory.

THE REPOLITICISATION OF RACE

The argument that race and immigration issues were 'repoliticised' in the 1970s could be quite confusing given that immigration was an issue that seemed to concern a large number of voters even after supposed depoliticisation had occurred in the mid-1960s. In fact, race relations policy was an explicitly political response to the 'problem' of immigration. Contained within the policy paradigm were measures designed to reduce the salience of the issue in order, from Labour's perspective, to lessen its vulnerability to populist exploitation of anti-immigration sentiment. Therefore, depoliticisation was largely an elite-level strategy – an agreement between the party's frontbenches – which never managed effectively to bind grass roots party members or voters to the policy framework. Repoliticisation occurred when Thatcher sought to capitalise on anti-immigration feeling and bring immigration back into the domain of two-party competition.

In the 1970s, as in the 1960s, Labour took a harder line on immigration when in government than it did in opposition. Labour opposed the Immigration Act 1971, but did not repeal it after winning the two general elections of 1974. This experience of Labour in government disillusioned many activists and helped prompt debates about internal party democratisation and policy change following the 1979 general election defeat.

The 1974-79 Labour government was forced by Thatcher to respond to the repoliticisation of immigration. In 1976 Home Office junior minister Alex Lyons was sacked for being too 'soft' on immigration. Labour also partially anticipated the Thatcher government's changes to British nationality in the British Nationality Act 1981. In 1977 a government white paper, *British Nationality Law: Discussion of Possible Changes*, proposed a distinction between British citizens and British overseas citizens for those in former colonies. These proposals made it difficult for Labour to oppose the main aspects of the 1981 Act.

Nevertheless, in the 1970s an anti-racist critique of race relations policy began to develop as Labour moved to the left. Labour members played a part in mobilisation against the NF. However, the NF also polled well in working-class areas where Labour was traditionally strong, and attracted Labour voters with its anti-immigration policies. This illustrated Labour's dilemma; namely, how to combat racism and consolidate support among ethnic minorities while, at the same time, not alienating white, working-class, anti-immigration voters. It was argued that race relations policy, with its emphasis on control of numbers, appeased rather than confronted racists, thereby neglecting the wholly legitimate interests of Labour's supporters from ethnic minority groups.

There was also evidence of increased registration and turnout among ethnic minority voters. In 1975 the Labour Party Race Action Group (LPRAG) was established to seek more effective representation of ethnic minority interests in the party. Important changes were occurring in the 1970s as people from ethnic minorities sought to exercise their political rights and questioned the unrepresentativeness of British political institutions.

A catalyst for this was a report by the Community Relations Commission into the outcome of the October 1974 general election which drew attention to the importance of 'ethnic marginals'.[1] In some seats the proportion of population of ethnic minority origin exceeded the majority of the winning MP, thereby (it was argued) making ethnic minority voters central to electoral success.

There were one or two problems with these findings. To begin with, ethnic minority voters tended to be strong Labour supporters, not floating voters whose switch from one side to the other could determine the result in a particular constituency. Also, it was argued that if Labour sought to increase its appeal to ethnic minorities it could lose support from the more numerous white, anti-immigrant voters. Despite these limitations, the report had the important political effect of drawing the party leadership's attention to ethnic minority voters.

Following the 1979 general election defeat the gulf between the right-wing party leadership and the left-wing grass roots became clear. The effects of left-wing influence were apparent in the development of anti-racist policies. These policies were linked to the rise of what has been called the 'municipal left', which was particularly influential in urban areas, notably London.

THE MUNICIPAL LEFT AND ANTI-RACISM

The race relations policy established in the 1960s involved decentralisation of responsibility for management of immigration-related issues. One aspect of this was creation of local Community Relations Councils. Another saw local authorities assume new responsibilities. Section 11 of the Local Government Act 1966 provided funding for local authorities to meet the special needs of ethnic minority groups. In addition, the Local Government Grants (Social Need) Act 1969 implemented the Urban Programme which, although not specifically targeted towards ethnic minorities, provided funding to parts of the country where immigrant settlement was high.

The emphasis on local solutions to anti-discrimination was made clear by an amendment to the Race Relations Act 1976 which gave local authorities responsibility to carry out their functions in order to eliminate unlawful racial discrimination and promote equality of opportunity and good race relations.

This legislation provided local authorities with the potential for anti-racist activity and coincided with development of the anti-racist critique of race relations policy by Labour's left-wing.

> The strategists of what has been called the 'municipal left' saw a commitment to, amongst other things, anti-racism, as a way of broadening Labour's commitment to egalitarianism beyond the more traditional left focus on class inequality.[2]

This involved attempting to recast Labour's electoral coalition to construct a 'Rainbow Alliance' based on what have been called 'new social movements'. This meant capitalising on concerns about gender inequalities, peace and disarmament, environmentalism, gay rights and anti-racism.

In 1978 Lambeth council was the first in the country to establish a race relations unit (run by Herman Ouseley, who now chairs the CRE). Some authorities were 'pioneers' as they devised new anti-racist strategies in areas such as personnel recruitment. Others were 'learners' which followed the actions of pioneering authorities. There were also 'waverers' which made statements of good intent but took little practical action. Finally there were 'resisters' which did not see the need for formal policies on race issues. Among these were left- and right-wing authorities. Liverpool's Militant-dominated city council derided the 'yuppy left' and preferred to focus on class inequalities.[3]

The best example of the municipal left in power was the GLC which, until its abolition in 1986, developed anti-racist policies. Its ethnic minorities committee engaged in research, consultation and grant distribution; 1984 was declared 'GLC Anti-Racist Year'. The left-wing GLC was a thorn in the side of the right-wing Conservative government because across the River Thames from the House of Commons the GLC developed a critique of Thatcherism. The Conservatives' allies in the tabloid press attacked the 'loony left'. Stories, many of which turned out to be untrue, were published about local authorities doing such things as rewriting nursery rhymes to make them anti-racist and banning black bin liners.

Also, following the 1983 general election defeat the new Labour leader, Neil Kinnock, was keen to enhance the electability of the Labour Party. This meant ditching many left-wing policies that were seen as contributing to the party's general election defeat. The party leadership was not keen to be associated with the actions of left-led local authorities. From the mid-1980s, the ascendancy of the Labour left in local government ended and was superseded by an emphasis on 'municipal entrepreneurialism' which, rather than developing a critique of capitalism, sought to promote partnerships with commerce and industry.

The development of anti-racist policies did however draw attention to the absence of ethnic minority political representation. In the 1970s there were very few councillors from ethnic minority groups and no MPs. It was thought that the absence of representation helped to generate racist policies. In the early 1980s Labour activists therefore began to consider the establishment of black sections to help remedy these deficiencies.

WHY BLACK SECTIONS?

Following Labour's 1979 general election defeat the gulf between party members and the leadership became increasingly apparent. One manifestation of discontent was the move to democratise and radicalise the party through groups such as the Campaign for Labour Party Democracy (CLPD). The party also moved to the left as the influence of 'Bennism' increased, particularly in constituency parties.

Labour's 1979 manifesto failed to reflect the increased radicalism of the grass roots membership. On race relations and immigration the manifesto made no pledges to repeal immigration legislation and contained only some low-key anti-discrimination proposals. Also only one ethnic minority parliamentary candidate was selected, in an unwinnable seat.

The party's defeat prompted the LPRAG to produce a report entitled *Don't Take Black Voters for Granted* which drew attention to the importance of Asian and Afro-Caribbean voters. In 1980 Labour's National Executive Committee (NEC) distributed an advice note among constituency parties on *Labour and the Black Electorate* which encouraged greater involvement of people from ethnic minorities. The report also criticised race relations policy for introducing discriminatory legislation, failing to tackle racism and not promoting effective equal opportunities policies.

From the early 1980s the campaign for black sections developed. Black sections were based on autonomous participation and representation within the party and would run on similar lines to already existing women's and youth sections. An important aspect of the debate about black sections was use of the term 'black':

> The black sections definition of black is essentially political, and based on people's direct, first-hand, experience of racism; it has to do with how they are treated by 'white' society, rather than what culturally distinct groups they belong to.[4]

One effect of this was that in the Haringey area of London, Cypriots were involved in black sections, yet in the 1991 census 95 per cent of Cypriots entered themselves as white. Also, as was noted in Chapter 1, it has been argued that many Asian people may not recognise themselves as 'black' and that the term is more representative of Afro-Caribbean identities.

A number of arguments were advanced in favour of black sections:
- The loyalty of ethnic minority voters was being taken for granted. Black sections would serve as a vehicle for increased participation and more effective representation of minority interests
- Labour was a major institution of a racist society and was itself likely to be institutionally racist
- One effect of institutional racism was lower participation in the Labour Party
- Explanations for lower participation and representation, such as apathy, were unsatisfactory
- Self-organisation in the party was the way forward and would help to radicalise the party.[5]

Black sections not only advanced a critique of racist society but also of a racist Labour Party. The party leadership showed itself unwilling to accept this argument because it could implicate it in an exercise in self-criticism that some did not feel was warranted and, anyway, would leave the party open to embarrassing attacks from its rivals, with potentially damaging electoral effects.

THE CAMPAIGN FOR BLACK SECTIONS

The first national black sections conference was held in Birmingham in June 1984, attracting nearly 300 people. By October 1984, 25 constituency Labour parties in the London area had allowed formation of black sections, despite their unconstitutional nature. Most black sections were created in London. In cities with large Asian populations, such as Leicester and Bradford, it was difficult to establish black sections because a politics of ethnicity based on religion prevented establishment of a black organisation attempting to unite diverse ethnic minority groups.

The 1984 party conference saw submission of 18 resolutions in favour of black sections with one opposed and seven amendments. Two resolutions were voted on. The first, calling for creation of autonomous black sections, was defeated by 5 427 000 votes to 500 000. The second, calling among other things for compulsory short-listing of black candidates for local and parliamentary candidate selections, if one applied, was defeated by 5 645 000 to 418 000.

In 1985 resolutions in favour of black sections were again heavily defeated. However, acting on the basis of a proposal from an NEC working party, it was decided to establish a Black and Asian advisory committee and appoint an ethnic minorities officer. Black sections boycotted the advisory committee as they saw it as palliative rather than an effective response to the issues raised.

The party leadership remained hostile to black sections. Leader Neil Kinnock, deputy leader Roy Hattersley, and shadow home secretary Gerald Kaufman voiced strong opposition. In their view black sections would lead to marginalisation and a form of apartheid within the party. Also, from 1985 black sections became more associated with Labour's left-wing. This was at a time when Kinnock was moving the party to the right. In 1988 black sections supported the challenge by Tony Benn and Eric Heffer for the party leadership and deputy leadership. Such strong support for the left at a time when it was weak contributed to the marginalisation of black sections.

There was also discontent within black sections about the lack of policy content in the black sections campaign, and fear that the organisation was serving as a vehicle chiefly for middle-class careerists who wanted to get a seat on a local council or to be selected as a parliamentary candidate. Black sections were created not only to foster increased representation, but also to facilitate development of a black, anti-racist, policy agenda involving a critique of racist society (and, by implication, racist institutions such as the Labour Party). It proved difficult to secure greater representation within the Labour Party while, at the same time, denouncing it for racism.

An illustration of this dilemma occurred in 1987 when the black sections chair, Sharon Atkin, was deselected as parliamentary candidate for the Nottingham East seat after she had condemned what she saw as Labour Party racism. Four other parliamentary candidates – Diane Abbott, Paul Boateng, Bernie Grant and Russell Profitt – dissociated themselves from her claims. In a joint statement they said that the election of a Labour government was more important than the creation of black sections.

At the 1987 general election four prominent members of black sections were elected as MPs. One effect of this was to remove from the black sections campaign some of its most capable performers. Even if they had wanted to, it would have been difficult for the MPs to balance constituency, parliamentary and party duties with an active commitment to black sections.

Following numerous defeats at party conferences a compromise measure was agreed in 1990. A Black and Asian Socialist Society was established, based on self-organisation with representation at all levels of the party. The society did not meet all the demands of black sections. For example, rights to nominate candidates in local and parliamentary selection contests were not granted.

THE SUCCESS OF BLACK SECTIONS?

To consider whether or not black sections were successful it is necessary to establish what their aims were. First, they sought to increase participation and representation in the Labour Party. Second, they sought to develop anti-racist policy agendas within the Labour Party which were more reflective of neglected black interests.

The black sections movement was successful in drawing attention to chronic under-representation of ethnic minorities and played a part in rectifying this, although under-representation remains. By 1987 there were four Labour MPs from ethnic minorities as well as more than 200 local councillors. In London, in collaboration with the GLC, black sections played an important part in campaigns to increase voter registration and electoral turnout. However, black sections membership remained quite small. A 1986 survey showed that there were black sections in about 30 constituency Labour parties, with some 1500 members.[6] A 1990 survey of Labour's membership found that about 1200 people, or 0.4 per cent of members, belonged to black sections. The 1990 survey also found that 3 per cent of Labour's membership were drawn from ethnic minority groups.[7] It has been argued that:

> As the movement became more centrally controlled – intent on promoting its own members within the Labour party, rather than on developing policies and organising the black communities – its grassroots support, never very strong, showed no sign of growing.[8]

The movement for black sections achieved some, though not all, of its aims with the creation of the Black and Asian Socialist Society in 1990. It was less successful in developing a black policy agenda. This was because it was hard to specify what such an agenda should contain, and how representative it could be of Britain's diverse ethnic minority groups. It also proved difficult to develop a coherent politics of race within the Labour Party while at the same time criticising the party as a racist institution.

It has been written that:

> It could be argued that the pursuit of black representation, and its success, have channelled black anger and militancy into the official political machinery and neutralised it. Black anger is rendered harmless because it is directed away from effective mobilisation against racism and directed towards bureaucratic political machinery.[9]

However, it is also worth asking whether black sections represented 'moderate', 'mainstream' political opinion among people from ethnic minority groups. If they did, fundamental discussions about the efficacy of participation in the formal political process emerge.

THE EFFECTS OF SALMAN RUSHDIE'S THE SATANIC VERSES

An illustration of the problems surrounding the notion of 'black' identities was illustrated by the response to publication of Salman Rushdie's *The Satanic Verses* in September 1988. Protests came from the Muslim community as the book was seen as blasphemous. However, legal redress was not available to Muslims as British blasphemy laws do not apply to Islam.

In December 1988 and February 1989 well-attended demonstrations took place in Bolton and Bradford, culminating in copies of the book being burnt. On 14 February 1989 the Iranian leader Ayatollah Khomeini issued a legal decree, or *fatwa*, condemning Rushdie to death for his blasphemy. These events led to an anti-Muslim backlash with particular concern expressed about Islamic fundamentalism. Muslims became another 'enemy within', with Conservative MP John Townend calling for deportation of Muslims who could not accept the publication of the book.

The official Labour line was to condemn the *fatwa* and support free speech, although MPs Max Madden and Keith Vaz, who represented areas with large Muslim populations, supported the protests. Black sections were faced with a particular dilemma. Bernie Grant MP argued that because the protestors were black, black sections should support them. This was met with counter-arguments:

> Yet these demonstrators were on the streets not as blacks but as outraged Muslim fundamentalists. Not all Muslims are blacks, and not all Muslims take the fundamentalist position. Why then should black Socialists give support to hardline religious leaders?[10]

Anti-Muslim feeling continued to grow during the Gulf war, during which some Iraqis and Palestinians were interned. The Rushdie affair made it apparent that notions of 'black' as a political colour fail to take account of cultural differences within the ethnic minority population. The mobilisation against Rushdie's book seemed distinct from the protest and anger channelled through Labour Party black sections.

LABOUR'S DILEMMAS

Labour has clearly experienced difficulty in formulating a consistent policy response to the 'problem' of immigration. In the 1960s Labour was central to the formulation of race relations policy. One reason for this was that it feared the electoral consequences of being outflanked by a Conservative party prepared to capitalise on anti-immigration sentiment.

In the 1970s, Labour's part in the manufacture of race relations policy was challenged. The party leadership became distant from an increasingly radicalised membership. An anti-racist critique of race relations policy condemned the bipartisan approach for making concessions to racism. At the same time, there was evidence of growing participation within the party by people from ethnic minority groups.

This participation was in spite of the adverse participatory consequences of race relations policy. The attempt to neutralise issues of immigration and race by extracting them from party debate served also to marginalise the concerns of people from ethnic minority groups. Increased participation in the Labour Party, particularly from the mid-1970s onwards, sought to make Labour more reflective of the interests of its ethnic minority supporters though greater participation and representation. This led to the debate about black sections, which although not set up in the form originally sought, did draw attention to the marked under-representation of people from ethnic minorities in British political institutions.

Because of the strong electoral allegiance of people from ethnic minorities to it, the Labour Party has played an important part in the participatory debates which are discussed in the next chapter. It is clear from an analysis of debates within and between the main parties, as well as from the way in which race relations policy was formulated, that a number of factors militated against ethnic minority political participation. In particular, race relations was not designed to encourage political participation of ethnic minorities. Rather it sought to decentralise responsibility for management of race-related issues to local institutions, and thus reduce the electoral salience of the immigration issue.

NOTES

1. Community Relations Commission, *The Participation of Ethnic Minorities in the General Election, October 1974* (CRC, London, 1975).

2. A Geddes, 'Asian and Afro-Caribbean Representation in Elected Local Government in England and Wales', *New Community* 20 (1993), pp43-57.

3. K Young and N Connolly, *Policy and Practice in the Multi-Racial City* (Policy Studies Institute, London, 1981), pp6-7.

4. S Jeffers, 'Black Sections in the Labour Party: The End of Ethnicity and "Godfather" Politics?', in M Anwar and P Werbner (eds), *Black and Ethnic Leaderships: The Cultural Dimensions of Political Action* (Routledge, London, 1991), pp63-83.

5. Ibid, p70.

6. S Ingle, *The British Party System* (Basil Blackwell, Oxford, 1987), p134.

7. P Seyd and P Whiteley, *Labour's Grassroots: The Politics of Party Membership* (Oxford University Press, Oxford, 1992), p229.

8. Sewell, op cit, p107.

9. K Shukra, 'Black Sections in the Labour Party', in H Goulbourne (ed), *Black Politics in Britain* (Avebury, Aldershot, 1990), p187.

10. Jeffers, op cit, p75.

7 POLITICAL PARTICIPATION

Political participation plays an important part in legitimating political institutions in democratic societies, and is often viewed as indicative of integration and acceptance of social norms and values. This chapter presents evidence of exclusion of ethnic minorities from the political process, and prompts questions about the representativeness of the British political system. The participatory questions analysed in the chapter must be viewed in the context of earlier chapters. Race relations policy decentralised responsibility for management of race and immigration issues to 'buffer' institutions at the local level, such as Community Relations Councils, which were not elected and not clearly accountable to the communities they were supposed to represent. In this sense, race relations was not a particularly participatory paradigm. The policy response was structured in order to neutralise what was seen as a potentially damaging and divisive issue, not to foster incorporation of ethnic minority interests. However, during the 1970s and 1980s increased voter registration, electoral turnout, party activism and numbers of candidates for both local and national elections were all witnessed. These increases have continued into the 1990s. Yet under-representation in formal political institutions, such as the House of Commons and local councils, is still apparent. It is therefore necessary to account for factors explaining both increased representation and continuing under-representation and exclusion.

PARTICIPATION AND REPRESENTATION

In theory all citizens have the same formal political rights. In reality they may not be equally able to exercise their rights. It is thus possible to draw a distinction between access to and utilisation of citizenship, and illustrate how certain groups – typically white, middle-class males – are over-represented in political institutions. It is also necessary to think about why this occurs. One explanation is that socio-economic inequalities adversely affect political participation and cause under-representation of ethnic minorities.

Lower participation has been linked to what could be called 'lifestyle' constraints. Factors such as unemployment and poverty may affect a person's ability to participate in the political process. People from ethnic minorities are more likely to be working class, lower paid and unemployed than are white people. Such factors have adverse effects on political participation and show the importance of understanding how participatory channels in liberal democracies are differentially available and differentially used, and how they relate to the effectiveness of democracy.

Politics was famously described by Harold Lasswell as 'who gets what, when and how'. We also need to consider 'who participates' to understand the organisation into the political process of some issues and the organisation out of others. If individuals are constrained from participating in politics as a result of social inequalities, then their interests may not be effectively represented.

This chapter pays particular attention to the formal political process, its institutions and the political parties that seek power within it. A concentration on formal participation should not lead to neglect of informal political activity. Indeed, political analysts increasingly draw attention to the importance of community politics, protest organisations and pressure groups as important participatory vehicles.

Figure 7.1 distinguishes between formal/informal and electoral/non-electoral participation. This schema takes into account participation in formal representative institutions such as the House of Commons and political parties (boxes 1 and 2). It also allows us to consider other forms of political participation. Community groups, for example, would appear in box 4, whilst 'buffer' institutions such as the CRC would fit into box 3.

Figure 7.1 Dimensions of political participation

1	Formal/Electoral	3	Formal/Non-electoral
2	Informal/Electoral	4	Informal/Non-electoral

It is also necessary to consider representation. This is a term which is frequently used but less frequently analysed. It is possible to say that MPs are *elected* representatives, but that they are not *demographically* representative of the population because there are very few women and people from ethnic minorities in the House of Commons. This however raises the question whether MPs should accord with a *mirror* model of representation and reflect the demographic characteristics of the population. In fact, there are problems with this view. It assumes that people cannot represent others if they do not share their characteristics. It may therefore encourage them not even to bother trying. It has been argued that mirror representation is flawed and, taken to its logical conclusion, could undermine the basic principles of representative politics.

> If men cannot represent women can white women represent women of colour, can Asian women represent Afro-Caribbean women? Can middle-class heterosexual able-bodied Asian women represent poor, disabled, or lesbian Asian women? Taken to its conclusion, the principle of mirror representation seems to undermine the very possibility of representation itself. If no amount of thought or sympathy, no matter how careful or honest, can jump the barriers of experience, then how can anyone represent anyone else?[1]

This does not mean that attempts cannot be made to make supposedly representative institutions, such as the House of Commons, more reflective of a greater range of social interests. In the 1992 general election only 60 women and six people from Asian and Afro-Caribbean minority ethnic groups were elected. Women comprise more than half the population but make up less than 10 per cent of MPs. Fewer than 1 per cent of MPs are from minority ethnic groups, even though they comprise 5.5 per cent of the population. Many people agree that such glaring inequalities should be corrected.

In the United States attempts at correction have been made through redistricting. (In Britain a similar process is the changes made to parliamentary constituency boundaries.) Redistricting can create constituencies with majority black populations from which it is thought more likely that a black representative will be elected. In countries with proportional representation (PR) and multi-member constituencies 'balanced tickets' can be presented by parties which are more reflective of social demography. In Britain, ethnically-based redistricting (or boundary changes) has not occurred, while the single member-based electoral system undermines the PR remedy. This means that there is a lot of emphasis on the candidate selection processes.

THE 'ETHNIC MARGINALS' DEBATE

In the 1960s and early 1970s the main political parties took little interest in the votes of Asian and Afro-Caribbean people. Indeed, the main concern seemed to be white, anti-immigration voters. Labour attempted to neutralise the immigration issue by introducing hard-line immigration controls, while at the 1970 general election Powell's anti-immigration campaign showed the electoral potential of the 'race card' by increasing the public's perception of the Conservatives as the anti-immigration party.

This neglect was partly remedied after the 1974 general elections when the CRC produced an analysis of the election results and pointed to the importance of so-called 'ethnic marginals'. The argument was that in 76 constituencies at the February 1974 election and 85 constituencies at the October 1974 election the majority of the sitting MP was smaller than the proportion of the population from minority ethnic groups. If ethnic minority voters were to withdraw their support from a particular candidate, they could unseat MPs.

The report had an important political effect at a time when the main political parties were engaged in intense competition for votes. It pointed out that in 13 of the 17 seats Labour won from the Conservatives at the October 1974 general election the ethnic minority population exceeded the majority of the victorious Labour candidate. Relatively small numbers of votes could make all the difference at a general election and the parties were keen to secure support from as many sections of the population as possible. However, it has been argued that the report was methodologically flawed and that 'ethnic marginals' were not as important as was suggested. Three criticisms are particularly pertinent.

First, the CRC report equated the ethnic minority population with the ethnic minority electorate in order to assess the effect on sitting MPs' majorities. However, the ethnic minority population was likely to be considerably bigger than the ethnic minority electorate as the latter was (and still is) disproportionately skewed towards younger age cohorts, some of whom would not be old enough to vote. In addition, levels of electoral registration and voter turnout were lower than average among ethnic minorities (Table 7.1). In the 1970s people of Afro-Caribbean or Asian origin were less likely to be registered to vote than white people. By the mid-1980s registration levels among Asian people were similar to levels among whites. However, registration amongst people of Afro-Caribbean origin remained lower. This was particularly noticeable among the 18-24 age cohort and was taken as evidence of alienation from the formal political process.

Table 7.1 Voter registration by ethnic group, 1974-79

	% registered 1974	% registered 1979
Asian	73	79
Afro-Caribbean	63	81
White	94	93

Source Z Layton-Henry, *The Politics of Immigration* (Blackwell, Oxford, 1993), p.106

Second, the report assumed ethnic minority voters were floating. In fact, they were strongly aligned with Labour. An array of socio-economic, historical and geographical factors help to explain this. Labour traditionally attracted support from working-class people and many immigrants and their descendants were working class. Immigrants from India were favourable towards Labour as it had supported Indian independence, while people from the Caribbean were reminded of strong Labour parties on West Indian islands. Patterns of settlement were also important. Many immigrants settled in inner-city areas run by Labour councils. Networks of support and dependence developed between Labour-run councils and ethnic minority communities.

Third, a party that sought to cultivate support among ethnic minorities could alienate more numerous white, anti-immigration voters. Thatcher's 'swamping' statement could in fact be seen as recognition of the electoral importance of such voters. These people were more likely to be floating voters than were strongly Labour-aligned ethnic minority voters. Thus, a political party that sought to attract support from ethnic minority electors in an 'ethnic marginal' could suffer an adverse reaction from white, anti-immigration voters.

VOTING BEHAVIOUR

In the 1970s and 1980s previously stable electoral alignments seemed to come unstuck. Notions of class dealignment were developed to explain decreased levels of support for Labour among some sections of the working class. However, ethnic minority voters remained strongly aligned with Labour. This alignment can be linked to social class, but alignment was also strong among middle-class people from ethnic minorities. This indicates that class-centred explanations are not sufficient to explain ethnic minority voting behaviour.

In the October 1974 election the CRC survey found that 81 per cent of people from ethnic minorities supported Labour, with 9 per cent supporting the Conservatives and 10 per cent the Liberals. The figures were similar in 1979 with 86 per cent supporting Labour, 8 per cent the Conservatives and 5 per cent the Liberals.

Table 7.2 analyses voting behaviour in the 1980s and 1990s and makes a distinction between voters of Asian and Afro-Caribbean origin. It is important to bear in mind that these figures are derived from opinion polls and the like, which means they can be prone to sampling error based on, for example, the small size of the ethnic minority population. It has also proved difficult to disentangle environmental effects such as patterns of settlement and housing from other factors prompting strong alignment to Labour.

Table 7.2 Ethnic minority voting behaviour in general elections, 1983-92

	Asian	Afro-Caribbean
1983		
Labour	82	88
Conservative	9	6
Alliance	9	5
1987		
Labour	67	86
Conservative	23	6
Alliance	10	7
1992		
Labour	77	85
Conservative	11	8
Lib Dems	10	6

Sources Harris opinion polls for 1983 and 1987; CRE for 1992

At the time, some suggested that the strong alignment with Labour weakened in the 1980s, as revealed by the dip in support for Labour among Asian people in 1987. It was argued that social and spatial mobility made some sections of the Asian population more amenable to the Conservatives. However, the CRE's 1992 general election survey found increased support for Labour among Asian people. A lack of strong empirical evidence on voting behaviour among minority ethnic groups makes some of these issues difficult to assess. However, it would seem fairly clear that strong Labour alignment remains. The next task is to assess explanations for this.

CLASS, COMMUNITY AND ETHNIC MINORITY VOTING BEHAVIOUR

It is important to make a distinction between analysis of ethnic minority voting behaviour and examination of the 'ethnic vote'. The latter could comprise a distinct ethnic minority policy agenda of concerns not shared by white voters. However, as Saggar points out, empirical evidence tends to suggest that, 'the ethnicity of black voters only serves as an additional influence on their political actions over and above that of a wide variety of non-ethnic factors'.[2]

Indeed, available evidence tends to suggest that ethnic minority voters share many of the concerns of white voters. They may order them differently, though this could be as much to do with alignment to the Labour Party as with any ethnic factors. Issues may also be perceived differently by ethnic minority voters as a consequence of the 'race agenda'. For example, although all voters may express a concern about education, people from minority ethnic groups may be more concerned about issues of multicultural education than are white voters.

Social class plays an important part in explaining ethnic minority voting behaviour. However, social class alone cannot explain the strong electoral alignment with Labour because middle-class people from ethnic minorities are far more likely to support Labour than are white middle-class people. A major study of voting behaviour in Britain concluded that: 'Perceptions of group interests or processes of group identification are more plausible explanations.'[3]

A 1980s study also found social class to be an important motivator of ethnic minority voters. It found class to be a particularly strong motivator among Afro-Caribbeans, 76 per cent of whom said that they voted Labour because 'it was the Labour party that supported the working class'. Among Asians, 64 per cent thought similarly. Ethnic factors were found to have explanatory value with 31 per cent of Asians, these respondents saying that they supported Labour because 'it was the party that supported blacks and Asians'. Only 7 per cent of

Afro-Caribbeans thought similarly. This has generated the conclusion that Asian voters could be lured away from Labour because they are not as tightly tied to it by class considerations.[4] But it is important to note that the supposed vulnerability of parts of the Asian electorate to parties other than Labour is often linked to appeals to notions of 'community' captured in issues such as family values, law and order, thrift and enterprise. The Tory MP Nirj Deva has argued that such values make sections of the Asian population naturally conservative and thus potential Tory voters. Yet, under the leadership of Tony Blair, Labour has also sought to emphasise 'community' values. Consequently, the Labour allegiance of many Asian voters may not be as vulnerable as some analysts have suggested, and Labour's appeal may well be couched in terms of both class and community and thus less susceptible to Tory encroachment than previously supposed.

CANDIDATES FOR PARLIAMENT

The previous chapter showed that there was growing pressure in the 1970s and 1980s for increased representation of Asians and Afro-Caribbeans in formal political institutions. Until 1987 there had been no black MP since Shapurji Saklatvala lost his Battersea North seat in 1929. In fact, the main political parties displayed marked reluctance even to field ethnic minority candidates. Since 1970, numbers of ethnic minority candidates have, however, increased (Table 7.3).

Table 7.3 Ethnic minority candidates for Parliament, and MPs, 1970-92

	Conservative		Labour		All parties	
Election	Candidates	MPs	Candidates	MPs	Candidates	MPs
1970	0	0	1	0	8	0
1974a	0	0	1	0	6	0
1974b	0	0	1	0	3	0
1979	2	0	1	0	12	0
1983	4	0	6	0	18	0
1987	6	0	14	4	28	4
1992	8	1	9	5	22	6
Total	20	1	33	9	92	10

Source J Lovenduski and P Norris, *Political Recruitment: Gender, Race and Class in the British Parliament* (Cambridge University Press, Cambridge, 1994)

Recent years have thus witnessed increased representation in the House of Commons. However, despite increased representation since 1987 under-representation remains. If the number of MPs were to accord with the size of the ethnic minority population in Britain, there should be about 35 MPs from ethnic minorities.

At the April 1992 general election three MPs of Asian origin and three MPs of Afro-Caribbean origin were returned to the House of Commons (Table 7.4).

Table 7.4 MPs from ethnic minorities elected, 1992

Name	Party	Constituency	Majority
Diane Abbott	Labour	Hackney North	10 727
Paul Boateng	Labour	Brent South	9705
Niranjan Deva	Conservative	Brentford and Isleworth	2086
Bernie Grant	Labour	Tottenham	11 968
Piara Khabra	Labour	Ealing & Southall	6866
Keith Vaz	Labour	Leicester East	`11 316

Five of the six MPs represent London constituencies, while Vaz represents an area with a large Asian population. Ethnic minority candidates have been less successful in areas with smaller minority populations. In a 1991 by-election Ashok Kumar was elected Labour MP for Langbaurgh in Teesside, an area with a very small ethnic minority population. He lost the seat at the 1992 general election.

Analysts of under-representation have paid particular attention to ways in which parties select parliamentary candidates. A plausible explanation of under-representation of ethnic minorities is offered by the 'supply and demand' model, which likens the candidate selection process to a market. The model then highlights deficiencies in the market which inhibit selection of ethnic minority candidates. These weaknesses mean that the market for candidates is far from perfect, and that inequalities pervade the process and present a fundamental challenge to selection procedures that are supposed to be open to people from all social groups.

On the supply side, it is argued that too few people from ethnic minorities come forward to be considered for selection. Party membership levels are low. A 1990 survey found only 3 per cent of Labour Party members were of Asian or Afro-Caribbean origin. A similar survey found that only 1 per cent of Conservatives were of Asian origin, while the number of Conservatives of Afro-Caribbean origin was so small that it was not picked up by the survey.[5]

In the selection round prior to the 1992 general election, only about 30 members of ethnic minorities appeared on the party's 'Approved List' of potential parliamentary candidates. On the Labour side, it has been estimated that about 3 per cent of people on the 'A' list of candidates are of Asian origin, as are 4 per cent of candidates on the less important 'B' list. The absence of systematic monitoring of the candidates lists makes it difficult accurately to assess total numbers of aspiring MPs from ethnic minorities. There does however seem to be a supply-side deficiency.

This supply-side weakness could be explained by ways in which the candidate selection process consumes aspirants' time and money. The 'lifestyle constraints' mentioned earlier based on class, income and (un)employment mean that some people are less likely to have the resources necessary to compete successfully. Evidence suggests that working-class people, women and people from ethnic minorities may be hindered by lifestyle constraints which make it more difficult for them to become parliamentary candidates. White, middle-class males are far more likely to have the necessary resources – such as time and money – and are clearly over-represented in the House of Commons.

It is also necessary to understand the interaction between the supply and demand sides of the market for parliamentary candidates. On the demand side, a principal constraint is incumbency turnover. Only about 25 per cent of seats become available at a general election, and competition for these seats is intense.

In addition, other factors constrain minority representation. For example, there is evidence of racism. This discrimination can either be explicit, such as in Cheltenham when the selection of John Taylor as Conservative candidate led to much-reported racist comments by one party member. It can also be implicit and based on, for example, the view that ethnic minority candidates lose votes. Evidence derived from a study of the parliamentary candidate selection process between 1987 and 1992 suggests that party selectors do have this perception (Table 7.5).

Table 7.5 Attitudes of party members towards the electoral appeal of candidates, 1987-92

Candidate characteristics	Conservative	Labour
Local	+3.8	+6.2
White	+3.0	+2.3
Middle class	+2.0	+1.4
Female	+0.5	+2.0
Male	+1.9	+0.9
Working class	+0.3	+1.6
Trade unionist	−3.0	+0.5
Black or Asian	−2.6	−1.8

Note Original question: 'Do you think that for your party in this constituency certain candidates would gain many votes, gain some votes, no difference, lose some votes?'. Mean calculated after recoding as follows: gain many votes (+10), gain some votes (+5), no difference (0), lose some votes (-5), lose many votes (-10)

Source P Norris, A Geddes and J Lovenduski, 'Race and Parliamentary Representation', in D Broughton, I Crewe, D Denver and P Norris (eds) *The British Elections and Parties Yearbook 1992* (Harvester Wheatsheaf, London, 1992), pp92-110

However, this impression of vote loss is not substantiated by empirical evidence. It was, for example, found that:

> The 1992 general election represents mixed results for ethnic minorities. The total number of candidates fell whilst slightly more MPs were elected. Conservative challengers seem to have faced a slight electoral penalty, although black Labour incumbents did well.[6]

The four Labour incumbents who stood for re-election in 1992 all witnessed large increases in their vote: a 19.1 per cent in share of vote for Keith Vaz, 18.5 per cent for Bernie Grant, 11.1 per cent for Diane Abbott, and 7.5 per cent for Paul Boateng. Many factors explain these rises, but at the very least they do provide a counter to the simplistic view that ethnic minority candidates are vote losers.

However one or two very well-publicised selections may influence selectors' perceptions. In 1970 a man of West Indian origin, Dr David (now Lord) Pitt, was selected to fight the Clapham seat for Labour. This was a seat Labour should have won. In fact, it lost the seat with a 10.2 per cent swing to the Conservatives which was double the national average. In 1990 John Taylor, a Birmingham-based solicitor of West Indian origin, was selected for the Conservative-held seat of

Cheltenham. His selection divided the local Conservative Association, and the party lost the seat to the Liberal Democrats on a 5.2 per cent swing which exceeded swings in neighbouring constituencies.

'LOCAL LADDERS'

Many MPs have gained experience as local councillors, and there is evidence that this is valued by parliamentary candidate selectors. Local elected office can serve as a mechanism for representation of local interests, as well as a training ground for people seeking to acquire the skills and experience necessary for parliamentary candidates.

A 1992 survey found that 342 out of 21 000 local councillors in England and Wales were of either Asian or Afro-Caribbean origin. The survey found that there were more ethnic minority councillors than at any other time, and that the rate of increase was high. There was, however, still under-representation. It was also found that:

- 52.3 per cent of Asian and Afro-Caribbean councillors were in London
- about 85 per cent represented the Labour Party
- about 70 per cent of local councillors from ethnic minorities were of Asian origin, compared to 52 per cent of the total ethnic minority population who are of Asian origin
- of the 342 local councillors only 6 per cent were women.[7]

Even though there is increased ethnic minority representation at local level, it is also important to consider its effect. There is little research evidence of the impact of councillors from minority ethnic groups on the operation of councils and the shaping of local policy agendas.

INFORMAL POLITICAL PARTICIPATION

The formal political system is not particularly responsive to the needs of Asian and Afro-Caribbean ethnic minorities. This chapter has so far chiefly paid attention to formal and electoral participatory processes, and has noted under-representation at both local and national levels. Formal methods of participation are not, however, the only channels available, and it would be wrong to focus entirely on them. Forms of political action focused on local ethnic minority communities are evident across Britain. It has been written that 'people have shrunk the world to the size of their communities and begun to act politically on that basis.'[8] In addition, national organisations have developed to counter racial discrimination and fascist/racist political movements.

Two forms of informal political participation can be contrasted by distinguishing between 'resistance' and 'brokering' groups. In the 1960s resistance groups, such as the Black Panther Party, linked discrimination faced by immigrants in Britain to liberation struggles around the world. They were influenced by the activities of black leaders in the USA, such as Malcolm X. In Britain publications such as *Race Today* and the *Black Liberator* published the work of leaders such as Darcus Howe and Linton Kwesi Johnson. It has been noted that:

> Attempts were made at every opportunity to discredit these protest organisations. They were portrayed as a threat to law and order and systematic attempts were made to weed out such 'undesirables'.[9]

In 1971 the so-called Mangrove Nine were tried on charges of riot, assault, affray and conspiracy, following disturbances at a march protesting against police harassment organised by the Mangrove Community Association in London. The accused were acquitted of the serious charge of riot, but convicted of minor offences.

One brokering group was the Campaign Against Racial Discrimination (CARD), established in 1964-65. This quickly ran into disputes about political alignment. Some favoured independence while others, including the chair Dr David Pitt, sought to align with Labour. Differences proved to be insurmountable, and CARD collapsed in 1968. One group formed from it was the Joint Council for the Welfare of Immigrants, which exists today and does much to publicise the iniquities of immigration and asylum laws, as well as aiding their victims.

In the 1970s there was also anti-fascist and anti-racist mobilisation to counter the NF. In 1976 Rock Against Racism and in 1977 the Anti-Nazi League were formed. Both played key parts in discrediting the extreme right among young people. They also organised demonstrations against NF marches. Some turned violent, as in Southall in April 1979, when a New Zealand schoolteacher, Blair Peach, was killed. Demonstrators blamed the Metropolitan Police's Special Patrol Group. The Anti-Nazi League and newer organisations, such as the Anti-Racist Alliance, have been active in the 1990s to counter increased extreme right-wing activity in Britain and Europe.

ISSUES OF PARTICIPATION AND REPRESENTATION

The depoliticisation implicit in race relations policy has clearly had adverse participatory effects. It has tended to marginalise the concerns of ethnic minorities and to close off participatory channels in order to 'take the heat' out of the immigration issue.

In the 1970s and 1980s people from ethnic minorities became more involved in the formal political process. Increased representation at local and national level took place, and there are now more councillors and MPs from ethnic minorities than ever. However, under-representation remains, and there is evidence that constraints within the political process hinder minority representation and prevent fuller incorporation into the political process. Increases in representation are likely to continue, but change in this regard, as in most areas of British politics, is likely to be slow. At the moment there seems only to be partial – some might say token – inclusion. A key test of British representative democracy is whether or not it can become more inclusive.

The next chapter examines the politics of immigration in other European countries. There are parallels to be drawn between British experience and that in other European countries, although there are significant differences in traditions of citizenship and inclusion/exclusion.

NOTES

1. Kymlicka, op cit, p140.
2. S Saggar, *Race and Politics in Britain* (Harvester Wheatsheaf, Hemel Hempstead, 1992), p139.
3. A Heath, J Curtice, R Jowell, R Evans, G Field and S Witherspoon, *Understanding Political Change* (Pergamon Press, Oxford, 1991), p113.
4. Z Layton-Henry and D Studlar, 'The Electoral Participation of Black and Asian Britons: Integration or Alienation?', *Parliamentary Affairs* 38 (1985), pp307-18.
5. P Seyd and P Whiteley, *Labour's Grassroots* (Oxford University Press, Oxford, 1992) and P Whiteley, P Seyd and J Richardson, *True Blues: The Politics of Conservative Party Membership* (Oxford University Press, Oxford, 1994).
6. P Norris, E Vallance and J Lovenduski, 'Do Candidates Make a Difference? Gender, Race, Ideology and Incumbency', *Parliamentary Affairs* 45 (1992), pp496-517.
7. A Geddes, 'Asian and Afro-Caribbean Representation in Elected Local Government in England and Wales', *New Community* 20 (1993), pp43-57.
8. P Gilroy, *There Ain't No Black in the Union Jack* (Hutchinson, London, 1987), p245.
9. T Sewell, *Black Tribunes: Black Political Participation in Britain* (Lawrence and Wishart, London, 1993), p42.

8 THE POLITICS OF IMMIGRATION IN EUROPE

In analysing the politics of race and immigration in Britain, an important distinction between access to and utilisation of citizenship rights was made. Clearly, formal possession of civil, political and social rights does not in itself ensure their effective utilisation. Across Europe access to, utilisation of and, indeed, the very meaning and nature of citizenship are also important questions. By addressing these issues it is possible to uncover important political debates about 'belonging' in contemporary Europe.

BRITAIN IN THE CONTEXT OF EUROPE

For this reason, developments in Britain should not be viewed in isolation. Europe is an immigration continent, and other European countries have also had to respond to immigration-related issues. However, in other European countries immigration has interacted with factors such as differing traditions of citizenship and nationhood to generate different responses to the 'problems' of immigration.

Paying particular attention to developments in France and Germany can illustrate the nature of these different responses. These two countries, along with Britain, have been the major receiving countries. Yet in all three responses to immigration-related issues have varied. Indeed, official German discourse does not even recognise it as a country of immigration. Instead, Germans refer to *Gastarbeiters* (guestworkers) and asylum-seekers.

Developments at EU level are also important. It has been argued that the acceleration of European integration in the 1980s and 1990s contributed to development of Eurocentric racism alongside ethnocentric (nationally-based) racisms. One aspect of this argument is that a 'fortress Europe' is currently being created. Proponents of this view contend that EU immigration policy excludes economically disadvantaged non-European, particularly third world, migrants who are seen as jeopardising the economic well-being and social integrity of EU member states.

'IMMIGRANT' AND 'FOREIGN' POPULATIONS IN EUROPE

Migrant labour was central to economic reconstruction of western Europe after the second world war. The economic motive that under-pinned much immigration to Britain was also evident in other Euro-pean countries. As western economies grew during the post-war 'long boom', there was a demand for labour which could not be met by indigenous workforces. This meant that migrant labour was central to sustained economic growth and high living standards in west European countries. In turn, migrant workers benefited because they enjoyed higher standards of living than they they would have experienced in their native countries. Many did however face discrimination.

There was a much stronger element of planning in other European countries' immigration policies than there was in Britain's. France, for example, had long been concerned about low rates of population growth which had been evident in the eighteenth and nineteenth centuries. These concerns were exacerbated as a result of the huge loss of life suffered during the two world wars. In order to rectify the population loss, France concluded 13 labour recruitment agreements with sending countries between 1946 and 1965.

Once it had finished absorbing about 12 million Germans displaced from Soviet bloc countries after the second world war, West Germany also recruited workers. It did so from southern European countries such as Portugal, Spain, Italy and Turkey. The basis of recruitment was that the workers would be a temporary presence – *Gastarbeiters* – not permanently settled immigrants. By 1973, when this form of recruit-ment ended, there were about 2.3 million *Gastarbeiters* in Germany.

In addition to the pursuit of active recruitment policies, some European countries had colonial ties which bestowed rights of free movement on inhabitants of former colonies. This was the case in Britain and France, which had colonies in North and West Africa, and the Netherlands, which had Caribbean colonies.

The economic downturn following the 1973-74 oil price increases did not lead, as some had expected, to migrant labourers returning to their countries of origin. Both France and Germany ceased recruit-ment of foreign workers after the economic slowdown. But migration continued as family reunification occurred, leading to de facto per-manent settlement and formation of ethnic minority communities.

Settlement raised new policy questions about how best to seek social integration of ethnic minorities.

A more recent development has been a large increase in numbers of asylum-seekers following the end of the cold war and the outbreak of civil war in the former Yugoslavia. The former allowed increased freedom of movement for people from former Soviet bloc countries. The latter led refugees to flee the violence. Traditional migration flows from the south – Africa and Asia – have been supplemented by increased pressure from the east.

Ironically, denial of free movement was a long-standing target of west European liberal democratic criticism of the totalitarian Soviet bloc. However, freer movement from central and eastern Europe, on top of movement from third world countries, has generated a number of problems for receiving countries. In 1972, about 13 000 asylum applications were made in west European countries. In 1988 234 000 were made. In 1991 the figure had increased to 540 000, with about half making an application in Germany.

In absolute terms Britain, France and Germany are the largest receiving countries in Europe, though Switzerland and Luxembourg are heavily reliant on migrant labour (Table 8.1). The figures shown here underestimate the size of immigrant-origin populations, as they do not include people who moved to countries such as Britain, France and the Netherlands from former colonies and therefore came as citizens not foreigners.

It is also interesting to note that Italy, which had previously tended to experience net emigration, has recently experienced an increase in its population of foreign origin. This is of relevance to later consideration of EU immigration policy because Italy, along with Spain and Portugal, constitutes the EU's southern external frontier. The ability of these countries effectively to police their borders is something about which countries like Britain have expressed doubts.

Many people classed as foreign in Table 8.1 may actually wish to acquire more permanent status in their country of residence. In order to do so they must satisfy the nationality and citizenship provisions of the country in which they are settled. Citizenship, in a formal sense, is a key indicator of who is seen as 'belonging' to a particular society and who is not. The modern conceptualisation of citizenship developed by T H Marshall links civil, political and social rights to citizenship as a vehicle for promotion of national integration. There are, however, major differences in provision between European countries.

Table 8.1 Population of foreign nationality in selected European countries, 1990

Country of residence	Pop of foreign nationality, 1990	% change 1985-90	% total population
Belgium	900 000	+7	9
Denmark	160 000	+37	3
France	3 580 000	+3	6
West Germany	5 240 000	+20	8
Italy	780 000	+85	1
Luxembourg	100 000	+6	28
Netherlands	690 000	+25	5
Great Britain	1 740 000	+7	3
Austria	410 000	+52	5
Finland	30 000	+55	0.5
Norway	140 000	+41	3
Sweden	480 000	+24	6
Switzerland	1 100 000	+23	16

Source J Haskey, 'The Immigrant Populations of the Different Countries of Europe: Their Size and Origin', *Population Trends* 69 (Autumn 1992), pp37-47

AUSLÄNDERPOLITIK IN GERMANY

Official policy does not recognise Germany as a country of immigration, even though about 25 per cent of Germany's population are 'immigrants' of one kind or another. One consequence of this is that many people who are permanently resident are excluded from German nationality and citizenship, leading to a German policy discourse of *Ausländerpolitik* ('foreigner' politics). Another important aspect of the German case is that the word racism is not officially used because of the Nazi legacy. Rather, Germans speak of *Ausländerfeindlichkeit* (hostility towards foreigners or xenophobia).

The current dilemma underlying German policy has been described as follows:

> a country which opened its arms to hundreds of thousands of ethnic Germans during the disintegration of the east and which was willing

to unify and take on responsibility for another 17 million persons at a record pace did not consider that the unification of Germany might be the opportunity to offer full, unambiguous membership to the 4.5 million foreigners (less than half are Turks and Yugoslavs) who had been over a decade or two working, paying taxes, increasingly born and schooled in the country.[1]

The German *Völkisch*/ethnic conception of citizenship and nationhood excludes people who may have spent their lives in Germany and be integrated into many aspects of the German 'way of life' but remain foreigners because they are not of German descent. It is also difficult, but not impossible, to hold dual nationality because it is thought that 'one cannot serve two masters'. This phrase illustrates the rather absolutist conception of German nationhood.

German nationality law has its origins in the nationality statute of 1913. Post-war German citizenship and nationality law maintained key aspects of the previous notion of German nationhood, with its emphasis on qualification on the basis of *jus sanguinis* ('blood' or descent). Article 116 of the constitution defines a German as a person who *de jure* holds German citizenship, is a spouse or descendant of people who were settled in the Third Reich before 31 December 1937, or is a refugee or deportee with German ethnicity *(Volkszugenhörigkeit)*. In addition, naturalisation is a lengthy and complicated process which relatively few 'foreigners' undertake.

Since the end of the cold war Germany has received from former Soviet bloc countries large numbers of ethnic Germans *(Aussiedler)* who are entitled to enter Germany and assume German citizenship. One irony of the *Aussiedler* policy is that many people have used a parent's or grandparent's membership of Nazi organisations as proof of German descent. This use of the Nazi lists means that ethnic Germans who had nothing to do with the Nazis find it more difficult to prove German descent.

Germany also had relatively liberal asylum laws, provided for by Article 16/2 of the constitution. In recent years there has been a huge increase in the number of asylum-seekers entering Germany. In July 1993 this prompted a tightening of the asylum laws which, among other things, deemed some countries of origin 'safe' and allowed asylum-seekers to be returned to them.

Three principal types of movement of people have contributed to post-war immigration into Germany:
- ethnic Germans
- guestworkers (recruitment ceased in the 1970s)
- asylum-seekers

Table 8.2 gives an indication of the increase in asylum applications and movement into Germany by *Aussiedler*. It has also been estimated that there are about 2-3 million more ethnic Germans 'sitting on their suitcases'. There has also been large-scale post-reunification resettlement as people from the former GDR have moved to western Germany. In the first six months of 1991, 238 000 people moved from east to west Germany.

Table 8.2 Migrants into Germany, 1985-91

Year	Ethnic	Asylum
1985	38 968	73 832
1986	42 788	99 650
1987	78 523	57 379
1988	202 673	103 076
1989	377 055	121 318
1990	397 075	193 063
1991	220 000	256 112

Source B Marshall, 'German Migration Policies', in G Smith et al (eds), *Developments in German Politics* (Macmillan, London, 1993), p249

IMMIGRATION AND POLITICS IN FRANCE

The 'Republican' model of French citizenship was defined by the revolution of 1789. France was seen as a political community which admitted newcomers on condition that they adopted the national culture. French nationality law was first defined in 1843 and enshrined the principle of *jus soli*, which meant that all people born in France could become French citizens. Social institutions such as the church, schools and army played important parts in processes of socialisation and definition of the French nation.[2]

France also developed elements of an imperial model of citizenship, similar to that which applied in Britain following the British Nationality Act 1948. France had colonies in north and west Africa, and bestowed rights of free movement upon those subject to French rule. Muslim immigration from Algeria in particular led to increased politicisation of immigration in the 1970s. Concern was expressed that Muslims would not be assimilable to the French way of life. A legacy of bitterness resulting from the Algerian civil war, which ended in 1962, also existed. The extreme right-wing Front National (FN) has played on these concerns with some success.

Recently, there has been much debate about French citizenship and nationality law. This culminated in reform of the Nationality Code in 1993, which removed the automatic right to citizenship held by children of foreigners. It replaced this with, among other restrictive measures, an act of affirmation – an expressed willingness to become French – for people aged between 16 and 21.

A key contrast between Britain and France relates to what is known in Britain as 'race relations'. Such a notion does not exist in French policy as the emphasis on integration means that official French discourse perceives the nation as 'temporarily multi-ethnic, but not as permanently multi-cultural'.[3] Special recognition for ethnic minorities could be seen as a form of apartheid.

In France and Germany similar objective socio-economic processes of, for example, economically-motivated migration leading to permanent settlement have elicited differing policy responses. In France the emphasis has been on assimilation. In Germany the discourse of *Ausländerpolitik* has developed. A principal reason for this is the interaction between immigration and different traditions of citizenship and nationhood. A further reason is the historical particularities of the French and German cases.

The French and German policy frameworks clearly contrast with British 'race relations' which, to a limited extent, could be seen as according with the principles of a *multicultural* model of citizenship. Multicultural citizenship, which has been most effectively operationalised in countries like Australia, Canada and Sweden, extends the Marshallian framework and 'redefines citizenship to embrace the right to cultural difference'.[4]

THE EXTREME RIGHT IN FRANCE AND GERMANY

Extreme right-wing political parties in both France and Germany have had some success in the 1980s and 1990s. However, when measuring their success it is necessary to consider what evaluative criteria to use. As was the case with the National Front in Britain, it is important to bear in mind not only the electoral performance of the extreme-right but also its effect on public opinion and government policy.

In Germany extreme right-wing activity has been constrained by the legacy of Nazism. In particular, the Bundesamt für Verfassungschutz (BfV), or Federal Office for the Protection of the Constitution, monitors extremist groups on the left and right and can recommend that anti-democratic groups be banned. Also, the 5 per cent electoral threshold which parties must cross if they are to secure representation in the German parliament was established expressly to prevent small and extreme political parties from gaining an electoral foothold.

These provisions have not stopped extreme-right parties enjoying some electoral success. In the 1960s the Nationaldemokratische Partei Deutschlands (NPD, National Democratic Party of Germany) had some prominence in local and regional elections with its anti-foreign workers platform. In the 1980s Die Republikaner (Republicans) and the Deutsche Volksunion (DVU, German People's Party) have also experienced a measure of electoral success. In 1989 the Republicans polled 7.5 per cent of the votes and gained 11 seats in the West Berlin House of Deputies. In the same year's European elections the Republicans gained 2 million votes and six seats in the European Parliament. All of these seats were lost in 1994 when the Republicans, wracked by internal disputes, failed to cross the electoral threshold. In the 1992 local elections the DVU gained 6.4 per cent of the vote in Schleswig-Holstein and 10.3 per cent in Bremerhaven.

Another worrying manifestation of extreme right-wing activity has been an increased number of attacks on foreigners. Many attacks have been in the former GDR, where resentment towards foreigners and asylum-seekers has been particularly marked. They have been linked to the social and economic dislocation caused by reunification, with asylum-seekers serving as a soft target for expression of anger and resentment. Following the fall of the Berlin Wall there was an enormous upsurge in racist violence across Germany which led, at its most extreme, to the murder of three children and two women of

Turkish origin following a firebomb attack on a house in Solingen, Nord-Rhein Westfalia, in May 1993.

In elections in France Jean Marie Le Pen's FN has consistently been the most successful extreme right-wing political party in recent times. The party grew quite rapidly in the early 1980s. In 1981 Le Pen was not even able to get the 500 signatures necessary to endorse his candidacy for the French presidency. However, in local elections in Dreux in 1983 the FN secured 17 per cent of the vote. In 1984 the FN picked up 10 per cent of the vote in European Parliament elections, returning 10 MEPs. In 1986, after the introduction of proportional representation, the FN secured election of 34 deputies. All but one of these seats was lost when the electoral system was switched back to a majoritarian system in 1988. In 1988 Le Pen picked up 14.4 per cent of the vote in the first round of the presidential elections. In 1995 he improved slightly on this, gaining 15 per cent of the vote, only 3.5 per cent behind former prime minister Edouard Balladur.

In the 1995 presidential elections Le Pen presented a blueprint for a new Sixth Republic to succeed 'decades of political decay'. A policy priority was expulsion of 3 million immigrants, at the rate of 1200 per day. The FN also advocated a 'French first' policy in allocation of welfare benefits and housing. Support for the FN in the 1995 election was identified as coming from an area to the east of a line from Le Havre in the north to Montpellier in the south. The FN polled particularly well in former textile and mining regions of the north and east such as the traditional strongholds of conservative catholicism of Alsace and Lorraine in eastern France.

Despite the clearly racist overtones of the FN's programme it has been argued that:

> It brings together many other social and political meanings besides racism. It appeals to a more populist than frankly racist electorate. Similarly, all that is racist in France should not be attributed to it.[5]

The FN does articulate a racist 'French first' policy, but combines it with a populist critique of the ruling political class. Support for the FN has been linked to four factors seen as creating a dualised French society with people either 'inside' or 'outside'. First, industrial decline has prompted socio-economic dislocation which has upset traditional social and political allegiances. Second, France has gone from being a 'universal nation' either colonising or overseeing the transition to democracy in former colonies to, in some cases, forms of 'provincialism or retraction which becomes a dark populist, xenophobic nationalism'.[6] Third, economic change has fostered cultural change which has generated tendencies towards individualism and self-interest at the expense of a broader concern for the social good. Finally, a crisis of the republican state has been identified. It is argued that the French state is losing its capacity to integrate and is thus failing to counter disintegrative social tendencies.

The FN has had some success in French local elections – in June 1995, FN mayors were elected in the southwest town of Toulon and the smaller towns of Orange and Marignane, near Marseilles. In Toulon, the FN mayor, Jean Marie le Chevallier, introduced a racist 'French-first' policy, which denied fair treatment to immigrants. In addition, local authority grants to organisations, such as Aids charities, were slashed. FN leader Le Pen believes in isolation units.

In both France and Germany there is evidence of some electoral success for extreme right-wing political parties. However, votes in elections are not the only relevant yardstick. In particular it is also necessary to analyse the effects of anti-immigration/'foreigner' political movements on mainstream political parties. In France, the success of the FN has helped to push centre-right politicians into taking a harder line on immigration. In fact, in the period between the first and second rounds of the 1995 French presidential elections Le Pen was referred to as a 'kingmaker'.

EUROPEAN UNION IMMIGRATION POLICY

Integration within the EU has led to 'pooling' of sovereignty in many policy areas as a way of devising common solutions to common problems.[7] Immigration is an area which has witnessed increased cooperation between EU member states, although policy emerges as a consequence of intergovernmental cooperation rather than through supranational policy integration. This means that member states largely act unanimously in the Council of Ministers, and that each member can employ a veto on policy developments it does not like.

The main impetus to EU immigration policy development has been the 1986 Single European Act, which made provision for the attainment of the 'four freedoms': freedom of movement of people, services, goods and capital in a single European market. A paradox of the liberalisation implicit within the deregulatory single market programme is that removal of internal frontiers is seen as necessitating tighter control of external borders.

Initially, governments cooperated in a way that can be characterised as 'informal intergovernmentalism' outside the control of supranational institutions such as the Commission and European Parliament, and also largely beyond the control of national parliaments. Attempts were made to establish common rules on asylum (the Dublin Convention) and external frontier control. However, problems with ratification of both these conventions illustrated the weakness of informal cooperation. It was also felt that such secretive policy development exacerbated the 'democratic deficit' which is held to exist at European level.[8]

EU immigration policy was thus increasingly formalised in the Treaty on European Union (TEU) negotiated at Maastricht in December 1991. The TEU established two intergovernmental 'pillars' which were inside the new 'Union', but were not incorporated within the supranational 'Community' system within which the Commission, European Parliament and Court of Justice have influence. One pillar dealt with foreign and security policy, the other dealt with justice and home affairs, including immigration policy.

Article K1 of the TEU defines three subject areas relating to immigration policy as matters of common concern:
- Article K.1.1 on asylum policy
- Article K.1.2 on rules governing the crossing of external borders of member states
- Article K.1.3 on immigration policy and policy regarding nationals of third countries:
  (a) conditions of entry and movement by third-country nationals
  (b) conditions of residence by third-country nationals, including family reunion and access to employment
  (c) means of combating unauthorised immigration, residence and work by third-country nationals.

The TEU also made provision for the creation of EU citizenship. To qualify as a citizen of the EU, and acquire the limited package of rights outlined in Article 8A of the Treaty, individuals must first be a citizen of a member state. Thus, EU citizenship is a right derived from national citizenship and third-country nationals, such as second- or third-generation Turks in Germany, are excluded from it.

Outside the formal structures of the EU, the Schengen Agreement has brought together ten countries frustrated by slow attainment of free movement objectives. They have agreed among themselves to attain free movement of people more quickly. The original Schengen accord was signed in the eponymous Luxembourg town in June 1985. It was not until 26 March 1995 that seven Schengen signatories abolished controls on movement of people to create 'Schengenland'. However, France quickly had second thoughts and 'temporarily' withdrew from the arrangement. Britain has remained resolutely opposed to removal of frontier controls, and has not participated in Schengen.

FORTRESS EUROPE?

As is the case with most EU policy, EU immigration policy reflects national policy preferences. In this sphere it has generated claims that a 'fortress Europe' is being created which seeks to exclude migrants from the prosperous European single market, and will only serve to exacerbate differences between rich and poor countries.

Defenders of EU immigration policy argue that the provisions of the TEU introduce a greater element of openness into policy development, and that this openness may well increase as a result of the review of the EU's treaty framework in 1996-97. They point to an evolutionary policy development that is drawing EU immigration policy progressively closer to accountable supranational institutions.

Against this, proponents of the 'fortress Europe' standpoint argue that greater openness should not be used to disguise the principal intent of policy, which they see as racist and exclusionary. In their view the policy framework seeks to exclude economic migrants from third-world countries. It is also argued that the development of EU immigration policy creates a policy which makes immigrants themselves the 'problem', and that this has unfortunate repercussions for permanently-resident third-country nationals, as well as citizens of EU member states from minority ethnic groups. In particular, problematisation of the immigration issue could legitimate the standpoints of extreme right-wing political parties, who advocate strict control and even repatriation, and draw them closer to legitimate political debate.

Another weakness of the EU immigration policy framework is that it contains no provisions to counter discrimination on grounds of race or ethnic origin. In 1989 the European Community's Social Charter did state that discrimination on the grounds of sex, colour, race, opinions and belief should be combated but, so far, no anti-racism provisions have been enacted at EU level. Reports from the European Parliament in 1985 and 1991 drew attention to the extent of racism in Europe and argued, among other things, for EU anti-discrimination legislation.[9] Again, this is an issue which could be addressed by the 1996-97 Inter-Governmental Conference which will examine prospects for reform of the existing EU treaty framework.

If trends over the past 40 years are anything to go by, increased policy integration in Europe is likely. If so, immigration will become an increasingly important part of the EU's policy remit. Many of the issues of citizenship and 'belonging' discussed in this chapter are likely to be 'Europeanised'. Given the close links between citizenship and nation states which exist, some wonder whether it is possible to develop a post-national European citizenship. If such citizenship does develop, it is an open question whether it will include minority ethnic communities or further extend the elements of exclusion that are evident across Europe.

IMMIGRATION AND POLITICS IN EUROPE

At first glance it is difficult to compare European countries of immigration. Differing traditions of citizenship and nationhood have prompted very different policy responses, including German exclusion, French assimilation and British race relations.

However, there are elements of commonality which can serve as the basis of comparative analysis. At a basic level, similar objective processes of economic/political migration have had a clear effect on many European countries. In addition, the development of EU immigration policy imparts a greater degree of commonality to EU member states' immigration policies than was previously the case.

It is also clear that issues of citizenship will continue to be important matters of debate in multi-ethnic European countries. Many people of immigrant origin, despite being permanently resident in European countries, are effectively excluded from citizenship because of restrictive nationality laws. In other European countries access to citizenship does not necessarily mean that legal, political and social rights can be effectively exercised. The issues of protection of cultural rights and operationalisation of a notion of multicultural citizenship in what is clearly a multicultural Europe also arise.

If European integration maintains its current trajectory, debates about citizenship and belonging are likely to be 'Europeanised'. Such a development has attendant dangers of construction of a 'fortress Europe', which would cause great harm to minority rights. These, and other issues, clearly demonstrate the importance and continued relevance of issues associated with immigration in contemporary Europe.

NOTES

1. C Wilpert, 'Ideological and Institutional Foundations of Racism in the Federal Republic of Germany', in J Wrench and J Solomos (eds), *Racism and Migration in Western Europe* (Berg, Oxford, 1993).
2. W R Brubaker, *Citizenship and Nationhood in France and Germany* (Harvard University Press, Boston, 1992).
3. S Castles and M Miller, *The Age of Migration, International Population Movements in the Modern World* (Macmillan, London, 1993).
4. S Castles, 'Democracy and Multicultural Citizenship: Australian Debates and their Relevance for Western Europe', in R Bauböck (ed), *From Aliens to Citizens: Redefining the Status of Immigrants in Europe* (Avebury, Aldershot, 1994), p9.
5. M Wieviorka, 'Tendencies to Racism in Europe: Does France Represent a Unique Case or is it Representative of a Trend?', in Wrench and Solomos, op cit, p55.
6. Ibid, p60.
7. A Geddes, *Britain in the European Community* (Baseline Book Company, Manchester, 1993).
8. A Geddes, 'Immigrant and Ethnic Minorities and the EU's Democratic Deficit', *Journal of Common Market Studies* 33 (1995), pp197-217.
9. G Ford, *Fascist Europe* (Pluto Press, London, 1992).

CONCLUSION

Debates about citizenship are clearly highly important in Britain and other European countries. However, citizenship is not just a formal and juridical term bestowing status upon individuals, usually in a national context. Rather it is a mechanism through which membership in a society can be expressed by exercising rights and performing duties. In some European countries access to citizenship is of great significance as a result, for example, of exclusionary nationality laws. In Britain, utilisation of citizenship rights is more strongly emphasised because many post-war immigrants came as citizens with the same formal rights as other British citizens.

DISTINCT ISSUES WITHIN THE POLITICS OF RACE

However, formal access to citizenship does not mean that rights can be fully exercised. The main focus of this book has been on political rights, but of equal importance are legal and social rights. Also, if a notion of multicultural citizenship is to be operationalised as a way of protecting minority rights and ensuring effective participation of minority groups in the political process, then the question of cultural rights is also important.

The policy framework of British race relations established at the level of national government did not concern itself with the political participation of ethnic minorities. Instead, as a result of decentralisation of responsibility for management of race-related issues to local and community level, ethnic minority interests were marginalised. The determined attempt to reduce the salience of the immigration issue in the 1960s largely excluded British citizens from ethnic minority groups from decision-making processes. Thus if we are properly to understand 'who gets what, when and how?' it is necessary to address the question of 'who participates?'.

Increased levels of representation at local and national level in the 1980s and 1990s should not disguise continued under-representation. This under-representation, and the exclusion from the formal political process of which it is a symptom, prompts a form of unequal citizenship

in Britain which is entangled with ideologies of supposed racial difference and reduces the effectiveness of British democracy.

THE IMPORTANCE OF THE EUROPEAN CONTEXT

Debates in Britain must be put in their proper historical context. It
is also becoming increasingly clear that they are linked to broader
European debates. Other European countries have experienced similar
processes of labour migration in the post-war era. Responses to immigration have, however, been affected by different ideas about citizenship and nationhood, as well as by the different histories of receiving
countries. It is for this reason that the three largest countries of immigration in Europe – Britain, France and Germany – have established
different policy responses. British notions of race relations are not
consistent with French experience, while Germany does not formally
recognise itself as a country of immigration.

Despite these major differences, which make any attempt to analyse
the effects of immigration on European countries in a comparative
context extremely problematic, there is an increasingly important
element of commonality. This is chiefly generated through development of supranational EU immigration policy. Those who are concerned about manifestations of unequal citizenship and racist exclusion in Europe should certainly pay a good deal of attention to
developments in the EU. In particular, if EU immigration policy development continues, then debates about democracy and accountability
– closing the so-called 'democratic deficit' – will become of increased
importance. Even for the newly-created EU citizens, participatory
channels in Europe are under-developed. For those excluded from
national citizenship and thus from EU citizenship, these channels are
even more remote.

If a strong, democratic and accountable EU is to be built – a people's
Europe – then it should be inclusive of all EU citizens whatever their
ethnic origin. It should therefore include people who are permanently
resident in European countries but are excluded from national citizenship because of restrictive nationality laws. An important first step
would be enactment of European legislation outlawing discrimination
on grounds of race or ethnic origin throughout the EU and applicable
to all people living in European countries, not just citizens.

Debates at European level increasingly affect national debates. It is important to be as careful in analysing EU policy development as in assessing British race relations. In particular, no policy framework should be taken as 'given'. Instead, assumptions upon which policy is based should be probed to guard against further development of a 'fortress Europe'.

British experience suggests that a policy which has at its heart tight control of numbers has unfortunate effects for domestic 'race relations'. Similarly, overly restrictive EU immigration policy will confound both the instrumental principle upon which it is built – free movement – and the loftier human rights principles that member states have signed up to through the European Convention on Human Rights. Analysis of the British experience also implies that pressure should be exerted for development of a European policy framework that is participatory and helps to counter both exclusion from citizenship and, once it is attained, the unequal exercise of citizenship that is apparent across Europe.

A BRIEF GUIDE TO FURTHER READING

The conceptual issues raised in Chapter 1 are discussed in John Rex and David Mason (eds), *Theories of Race and Ethnic Relations* (Cambridge University Press, Cambridge, 1976), Robert Miles, *Racism* (Routledge, London, 1989) and Michel Wieviorka, *The Arena of Racism* (Sage, London, 1995).

There are three particularly good general sources on the politics of immigration, race and racism in Britain. Zig Layton-Henry, *The Politics of Immigration* (Blackwell, Oxford, 1992) and Shamit Saggar, *Race and Politics in Britain* (Harvester Wheatsheaf, Hemel Hempstead, 1992) are particularly strong on party responses to immigration and ethnic minority participation in the formal political process. John Solomos, *Race and Racism in Britain*, second edition (Macmillan, London, 1993), provides a more sociologically-orientated account which gives considerable attention to theories of race and racism.

Also worth consulting on the politics of race and immigration in Britain are Muhammad Anwar, *Race and Politics* (Tavistock, London, 1986), Terri Sewell, *Black Tribunes: Black Political Participation in Britain* (Lawrence and Wishart, London, 1993), and Harry Goulbourne (ed), *Black Politics in Britain* (Avebury, Aldershot, 1990).

There are very few general sources on immigration in Europe. Stephen Castles and Mark Miller's, *The Age of Migration* (Macmillan, London, 1993) has a strong, though not entirely, European focus. John Wrench and John Solomos (eds), *The Politics of Racism and Migration in Western Europe* (Berg, Oxford, 1993) contains much of interest. Zig Layton-Henry (ed), *The Political Rights of Migrant Workers in Western Europe* (Sage, London, 1990) provides information on political rights in west European countries.

A number of journals focus on race, racism and immigration. These include *Ethnic and Racial Studies, Race and Class, New Community, Patterns of Prejudice, Immigrants and Minorities*, and *The International Migration Review*. Other more general political science journals, such as *Political Studies, West European Politics* and *Parliamentary Affairs* sometimes contain articles about issues raised in this book.

Finally, the Runnymede Trust produces a regular bulletin entitled *Race and Immigration,* and the Institute of Race Relation's European Race Audit reports on racism in European countries.

INDEX

IN THE SAME SERIES

Liam Byrne, *Local Government Transformed*

Clyde Chitty, *The Education System Transformed*

Steven Fielding, *Labour: Decline and Renewal*

Andrew Geddes, *Britain in the European Community*

Ian Holliday, *The NHS Transformed, second edition*

Dermot Quinn, *Understanding Northern Ireland*

Martin J Smith, *Pressure Politics*

Stephen C Young, *The Politics of the Environment*